DISCARD

W9-AYO-851

Eyewitness
JUNGLE

Medicinal
calabar beans
*Physostigma
venenosum*

Eyewitness
JUNGLE

White-lipped
tree frog
Litoria infrafrenata

Written by
THERESA GREENAWAY

Photographed by
GEOFF DANN

*Clerodendrum
splendens*

Climbing fern
Leptochilus decurrens

Medicinal
Heckel
chewstick
Garcinia kola

Stone ax
(Guyana)

DK

DK Publishing, Inc.

Spear (Guyana)

LONDON, NEW YORK, MELBOURNE,
MUNICH, and DELHI

Pacu
Colossoma oculus

Cassava
squeezer
(Guyana)

Project editor Miranda Smith
Art editors Andrew Nash & Sharon Spencer
Managing editor Simon Adams
Managing art editor Julia Harris
Production Catherine Semark
Picture research Kathy Lockley
Research Céline Carez

REVISED EDITION
Managing editor Andrew Macintyre
Managing art editor Jane Thomas
Category publisher Linda Martin
Art director Simon Webb
Editor and reference compiler Sue Nicholson
Art editor Andrew Nash
Production Jenny Jacoby
Picture research Deborah Pownall
DTP designer Siu Yin Ho

U.S. editor Elizabeth Hester
Senior editor Beth Sutinis
Art director Dirk Kaufman
U.S. production Chris Avgherinos
U.S. DTP designer Milos Orlovic

This Eyewitness ® Guide has been conceived by
Dorling Kindersley Limited and Editions Gallimard

This edition published in the United States in 2004
by DK Publishing, Inc., 375 Hudson Street, New York, NY 10014

04 05 06 07 08 10 9 8 7 6 5 4 3 2 1

Copyright © 1994, © 2004, Dorling Kindersley Limited

A catalog record for this book is available
from the Library of Congress.

ISBN 0-7566-0694-2 (HC) 0-7566-0693-4 (Library Binding)

Color reproduction by Colourscan, Singapore
Printed in China by Toppan Printing Co. (Shenzhen), Ltd.

Passionflower
Passiflora sp.

Serpent carved
paddle (Papua,
New Guinea)

Discover more at

www.dk.com

Contents

Red-kneed tarantula
Brachypelma smithi

What is a rain forest?

TROPICAL RAIN FORESTS are perhaps the least understood and most valuable of the world's ecosystems. They are structurally complex, ages old, and have a climate that allows year-round growth. They contain a larger diversity of plants and animals than anywhere else on Earth – for example, there are 20–100 different kinds of trees in one acre of rain forest alone. These jungles have three layers – an evergreen canopy in the middle, a layer of smaller plants on the forest floor, and towering above the canopy, scattered taller trees known as emergents. The speed at which the vegetation grows and fills any gap or forest clearing impresses modern visitors as much as it did the early explorers. Rain forests all around the world are amazingly uniform in many respects. Similar niches on different continents have been filled by species that look alike but are unrelated.

COLOR IN THE CANOPY
Splashes of color in the canopy may indicate that a tree has burst into flower. It is just as likely that a flush of red, orange, pink, or white new leaves has unfurled.

NORTH AMERICA

RUSSIA

Tropic of Cancer

INDIA

AFRICA

Equator

SOUTH AMERICA

Tropic of Capricorn

AUSTRALIA

☐ *Rain forest area*

Palm tree

Undergrowth

WARM AND VERY WET
Tropical rain forests are found in permanently wet, warm areas near the equator. There are at least 60 in (1,500 mm) of rain a year, with little or no dry season. The rain falls almost every day, in torrential downpours of huge raindrops. The average temperature is around 77°F (25°C), and there is little seasonal variation.

THE FOREST FLOOR
Swamp forest soils are regularly enriched by silt-laden floodwaters. Away from flooded areas, much of the lowland forest has surprisingly poor, infertile soils called oxisols. Nutrients are locked up in living plants and animals until released by organisms such as termites and fungi.

Tall emergent tree

Canopy

Liana

Young sapling

At the top

Green-winged
macaw

Black-and
white-colobus

Queen Alexandra's
birdwing

Forest canopy

Cuvier's toucan

White–lipped
tree frog

Forest floor

Red–kneed
tarantula

RAIN FOREST IN THREE STORIES
This model shows many of the features shared by all
lowland tropical rain forests. The trees have straight trunks,
with no branches for much of their height, and are supported by
buttress roots. Lianas, or climbing plants, twine up the trees, or begin life
lodged in the canopy and send roots down to the earth below. At ground
level, a luxuriant growth of plants springs up wherever the light reaches.

Tropical forests

THERE ARE SEVERAL different types of tropical forest. Lowland rain forest covers the greatest area and is found in the warm, wet lowlands where there is little or no dry season. Tropical mountainsides are thickly forested. At altitudes over 3,000 feet (900 m), lowland rain forest changes to montane or high-altitude forest, which is divided into lower montane, upper montane, and cloud forest. Cloud forest begins at heights above 10,500 feet (3,200 m). At this altitude the stunted, gnarled trees are shrouded in mist and covered with mosses and liverworts. Sometimes the division between rain forest types is clear, but often two rain forest types merge so there is no clear boundary. Seasonal or monsoon forest – not technically rain forest – also has heavy rainfall, but there is a dry season of three months or longer, during which the trees shed their leaves. Lianas and epiphytes cannot survive these dry conditions.

MONTANE FOREST
In Malaysia, lowland rain forest gives way to lower montane forest at altitudes of about 3,000 ft (900 m). The climate is cooler but still moist. There is dense tree cover, but the height of the canopy gets lower and lower. The trees have smaller leaves, and tree ferns are abundant, as are magnolias, rhododendrons, myrtles, and laurels.

CLOUD FOREST
At higher altitudes, a permanent heavy mist envelops the forest. The climate of cloud forests, such as this reserve in Ecuador, is cool and very damp. Moisture in the mists condenses on the surface of the leaves and constantly drips from them. Mosses and liverworts cover everything with a spongy blanket. Because of the lower temperatures, the leaf litter decomposes very slowly. A thick layer builds up on the ground, eventually turning into peat.

Height at which montane forest replaces lowland forest is variable

Montane

Lowland

Mangrove

RAIN FOREST LEVELS
Lowland rain forest can extend down to the coast. Wherever conditions allow (p. 9), mangrove forest grows along the coast and in river estuaries. With every 330 ft (100 m) increase in altitude, there is a drop in temperature of about 1.1°F (0.6°C).

LOWLAND RAIN FOREST
The structure of this lowland rain forest in Peru is clearly visible from the Rio de Los Amigos. In the foreground, young climbers, ferns, and saplings flourish in the higher light levels beside the river. A cycad, a remnant of a truly ancient group of plants, also grows in this clearing. Tall palms make up a large proportion of the canopy. The umbrella-shaped crowns of the huge emergent trees tower above the canopy.

Scarlet ibis
Eudocimus ruber
(South America)

LIVING IN A SWAMP
Perhaps the most spectacular inhabitant
of South American mangrove swamps
is the scarlet ibis. It nests and roosts in
large colonies. By day, it feeds in tidal
mudflats or in the shallow waters of
lagoons or beaches, probing for shellfish
and worms with its long bill. As dusk
approaches, a whole flock wheels and
circles against the sky before flying
into the mangroves to roost.

STILT ROOTS
The palm *Verschaffeltia splendida*
is found naturally only in the
rain forests that cover the steep
hillsides of the Seychelles, in
the Indian Ocean. There, the
wet, rocky ground has a thin
layer of soil. Thick stilt
roots grow out from the
lower part of the trunk.
They help anchor the
palm more firmly on
this difficult terrain.

*Verschaffeltia
splendida*
(Africa)

MANGROVES
Deep layers of mud and silt accumulate along
sheltered tropical coastlines and in river estuaries.
A number of different kinds of trees, collectively
known as mangroves, colonize these muddy
shores and form swampy forests. The mud
and warm, shallow seawater are very low
in oxygen. So that the roots can breathe,
mangroves have pneumatophores, special
roots that stick up above the mud and
take in oxygen from the air through large
pores called lenticels. The *Rhizophora*'s
pneumatophores (above) grow in a
tangle of arches; others are like
knobbly knees or narrow spikes.

*New stilt root
growing out
from trunk*

*Splayed-out stilt
roots improve
anchorage*

At the top

T ALL EMERGENT TREES tower above the rest of the jungle canopy, a few reaching heights of 200-230 ft (60-70 m). These scattered trees have straight trunks, often buttressed at the base, and a cauliflower-shaped crown. It is hotter and drier at the top of the canopy, and the temperature and humidity vary greatly. The trees are also much more windblown, and the fruit or seeds of some species are dispersed by the moving air. Many emergent trees are leafless for short periods of time, but seldom shed alltheir leaves at once. The epiphytes that live on the boughs of these trees include drought-resistant species of bromeliads, lichens, and cacti.

MONKEY BUSINESS
The striking black-and-white colobus monkey lives at the top of the jungle, feeding on leaves.

Sun conure
Aratinga solstitialis
(South America)

FLYING FORAGER
Conures live in noisy flocks high up in the treetops. They fly restlessly from tree to tree, feeding on flower buds, fruits, seeds, and insects.

PENANG FOREST
Tualang trees (*Koompassia excelsa*) often reach 230 ft (70 m) – but a 285 ft (87 m) tualang holds the record for the tallest broad-leaved rain forest tree. Malaysians believe that spirits live in these trees.

Leaves have a waxy surface

GREEN SHADES
The tall canopy tree *Carapa guianensis* belongs to the mahogany family and is found predominantly in swampy or seasonally flooded parts of the forest. Mature trees may produce 300 or more large corky fruits that split into four segments, each containing two or three large seeds— most of which are eaten by animals.

Carapa guianensis
(Central and South America)

EAGLE-EYED
The harpy, one of the world's largest eagles, leaves its post in a tall emergent tree to swoop with speed and agility through the canopy. With its strong legs and immense talons (its feet are the size of a man's hands), it snatches howler monkeys or sloths, wrenching them free from a tightly grasped branch. Harpy eagles use the same nest site every year. They build a bulky nest of sticks lined with leaves and fur in the boughs of an emergent kapok tree, 165 ft (50 m) or so above the ground.

Harpy eagle
Harpia harpyja
(Central and South America)

Rhipsalis baccifera
(South America)

Small white fruit

CACTUS AT THE TOP
Its fleshy, leafless stems mean that this epiphytic cactus can survive the long, hot dry spells between downpours. The small white fruits have a sticky pulp that helps them adhere to the bark.

Young developing leaf

Abarema idiopoda
(Central America)

Bi-pinnate leaf

LEAF DIVISION
Rain forest trees have large leaves. These leaves are either simple, with a smooth outline and a waxy surface, or compound, when the leaf is divided into separate leaflets. *Abarema* is bi-pinnate – its leaves are twice divided and have small leaflets. *Carapa and Abarema* are leafless for brief periods, when there is a dry spell, or the tree is flowering.

11

Forest canopy

LIFE IN THE CANOPY
This male tawny rajah (*Charaxes bernardus*) is one of many kinds of butterfly that may spend their entire life cycle up in the forest canopy.

IN THE CANOPY of a rainforest, 80-150 ft (25-45 m) above the ground, it is always green and leafy. The crown of each tree is taller than it is broad, making a sun-speckled layer 20-23 ft (6-7 m) thick. This leafy roof shields the ground and absorbs most of the sunlight. It also lessens the impact of heavy rainfall and high winds. The teeming life of a jungle canopy is only glimpsed from below. Some creatures are so adapted to their treetop existence that they seldom, if ever, descend to the forest floor. It is difficult even to match up fallen fruits or flowers with the surrounding tree trunks. Many species were totally unknown – or their numbers grossly underestimated – before walkways strung up in the canopy allowed biologists to find out what life was really like in the treetops.

SAFE ASLEEP?
Canopy-dwelling creatures such as this silky or pygmy anteater (*Cyclopes didactylus*) need to cling tightly to the branches. Sharp claws and a long prehensile (grasping) tail are adaptations shared by unrelated canopy animals.

REACHING THE HEIGHTS
Lianas are plants that need a lot of light, which they have to compete for against tall rainforest trees. By using these trees for support, the lianas do not invest energy and materials in a thick trunk of their own. Instead, their slender climbing stems reach the canopy, and the light, very quickly. Once up among the branches, they loop through the tree tops, growing leaves, flowers, and fruit.

Liana
Clerodendrum splendens
(Africa)

White-lipped tree frog
Litoria infrafrenata
(Australasia)

STICKY-TOED TREE TRAVELER
To avoid the hottest part of the day, thin-skinned tree frogs hide in damp leafy crevices among canopy epiphytes. The smaller tree frogs may spend their entire lives in the canopy, even breeding in the reservoirs of water trapped by bromeliad leaves. Others, such as this white-lipped tree frog, laboriously make their way down to forest pools to mate and spawn. Long legs and sticky toe pads enable them to climb with complete ease.

Cecropia glaziovii
(Central and South
America)

CANOPY FOLIAGE
The large leaves of lowland rainforest trees may
be simple in shape, or divided into leaflets or
lobed. The canopy remains leafy all year, but
within it, some trees shed their foliage
for short intervals – sometimes
as little as a few days.
Leaf-fall usually coincides
with the driest time
of the year, but it
is not always
synchronized,
even in trees
of the same
species.

Large lobed leaf

DRIP-TIPS
This typical rain forest leaf has
a shiny, waxy surface, and it
is drawn out into a narrow
point, or drip-tip. Both these
features are designed to
encourage rainwater to run
off quickly. This prevents
the growth of tiny algae
and liverworts.

FLEETING BEAUTY
Completely invisible from the ground,
epiphyte-laden boughs are like treetop
gardens. Of all the different plants
perched on these branches,
orchids are among the
most fascinating. The
perfect white orchids
(right) last just
one day.

One-day orchid
Sobralia sp.
(Central America)

Ficus religiosa
(Southeast Asia)

INSECT LIFE
Only some canopy insects have been
classified and named, like this click
beetle (*Chalculepidium* sp.). Even
then, little is known about them.

13

The forest floor

THE AIR NEAR the shady forest floor is still, hot, and humid. Only about two percent of the light reaching the canopy penetrates the thick blanket of foliage. This dim light inhibits the growth of tree seedlings and other light-demanding plants. In the deepest jungle, the ground is a maze of roots littered with fallen leaves, twigs, and branches. When a tree crashes down, the scene is very different – the extra light allows an upsurge of saplings, herbaceous plants, and lianas. Rates of growth are impressive; giant bamboo grows 9 in (23 cm) a day.

FOREST FUNGI
Bacteria, molds, and fungi such as this *Marasmius* grow quickly in the humid conditions of the forest floor. A mass of fungal threads called a mycelium takes nutrients from the litter of dead leaves, and the brightly colored toadstools produce spores.

SHADE LOVER
Each long-stalked leaf of *Alocasia thibautiana* has silvery veins on top and is purple underneath. Clumps of these shade-loving aroids can grow in the gloomiest parts of Southeast Asian jungles – on the forest floor, beside streams, and even in the entrances of limestone caves.

A SPLASH OF COLOR
A luxuriant growth springs up wherever there is enough light. Heliconias, with their bright red flowerheads, are widespread in Central American jungles.

TRAPPING LIGHT
The leaves of *Fittonia* contain red pigments that trap the dim light that reaches the forest floor. Amerindian tribes use the plant to treat a variety of ailments.

Diplazium proliferum
(Southeast Asia)

Fittonia albivenis
(South America)

FLOURISHING
Ferns thrive best where it is warm and damp. Many tolerate low light levels, so they are abundant on the jungle floor. This fern produces bulbils on its fronds that will sprout and take root, either when they are knocked off or when the frond dies.

BURROWING WORM
The black-and-white amphisbaenid (*Amphisbaena fuliginosa*) is neither a lizard or a snake. It is a wormlike reptile that lives in burrows in the damp soil and leaf litter of the forest floor. It feeds on worms and other invertebrates, detecting prey by touch.

Banded pitta
Pitta guajana
(Malaysia)

BROWSING BIRD
Using its good eyesight and sense of smell, the pitta forages for snails, ants, and other insects in the leaf litter.

BUTTRESS ROOTS
These enormous roots are characteristic of lowland tropical rain forest, where soil is thin or subject to flooding. The curving shapes rise from lateral roots. Buttress roots may spread up the trunk to 30 ft (9 m), forming supporting wings of particularly hard wood.

In the water

THE RAIN FOREST is awash with water. It drips from the leaves, collects in puddles, runs down mountainsides, and eventually drains into huge, meandering rivers. The Amazon is the largest river of all – together with its tributaries, which number 1,000 or more, it holds two-thirds of the world's fresh water. This vast water system supports an incredible diversity of life. It contains around 5,000 species of freshwater fish, and there may be another 2,000 that have yet to be discovered. Where rain forest rivers flood, they spread nutrient-rich silts over the surrounding land, creating swamp forests. When they join the sea, more silt is deposited in estuaries and deltas, contributing towards mangrove swamps.

WELL CAMOUFLAGED
Lurking immobile in shallow water, the craggy carapace of the matamata (*Chelus fimbriatus*) looks like a rock. This Amazonian turtle has nostrils at the tip of its long, uptilted snout which is used like a snorkel as it lies in wait for prey.

Leaf

Epidermis

Air-filled spongy tissue

Petiole

WATER HYACINTH
To keep the water hyacinth afloat, and the right side up, the petiole (base) of each leaf stalk is swollen into an air-filled float. Cutting this in half reveals that each float is made up of a mass of air-filled spongy tissue. The leaf and stem are encased in a smooth, tough skin, called the epidermis.

RUNNING ON WATER
The Jesus Christ lizard, or basilisk, runs using its tail to balance itself. It has scales and a flap of skin on its hind toes to increase surface area, so it can run on *water* to chase prey or escape danger.

Long tail used as extra leg on land

Large back feet stop lizard sinking on water

Jesus Christ lizard
Basiliscus basiliscus
(Central America)

Pacu
Colossoma oculus
(South America)

FRUIT-EATING FISH
The varzea and the igapo are two areas of swamp forest flooded every year by the Amazon. Fruits falling from palms and other trees attract fish such as the pacu.

Water hyacinth
Eichhornia crassipes

DANGER IN THE WATER
Armed with fearsome rows of sharp, triangular teeth, the predatory piranha is dangerous only in the dry season, when water levels are low and the fish gather in schools of 20 or more. By feeding collectively, the fish are able to tackle large animals, although their usual prey is other fish, mollusks, fruits, or seeds.

Piranha
Serrasalmus niger
(South America)

FLOATING PLANT
The water hyacinth (above) floats with its feathery roots dangling down into the water. The plants grow very quickly, forming large rafts on the surfaces of lakes and slow streams. Smaller clumps are dispersed by the wind, blown along like small, unsinkable sailboats.

Green anaconda
Eunectes murinus gigas
(South America)

*Smooth, shiny scales keep
friction to a minimum
when swimming*

DANGER ON THE RIVERBANK
Few carnivores would tackle a large anaconda
moving lazily along the river's edge. Anacondas stay
close to swamps or streams, and they can climb trees.
Exceptional individuals have been recorded at 30 ft
(10 m) or more, but most anacondas are smaller. They
are excellent swimmers, preying on animals that come
to the water to drink, and killing their victims by
constriction and drowning. Younger anacondas are
more likely to be preyed on, but they can use their
swimming skills to escape. The females
give birth to 9-in (23-cm)-long live
young in the water.

*Underside
yellow with
black markings*

*Black blotches break
up outline and are a
good camouflage*

*Broad leaves
to absorb
sunlight*

*Large gill chamber fills with
water so oxygen from the
water can be used to breathe*

Mudskipper
*Periophthalmus
barbarus*

SWAMP PLANT
Air spaces in the leaves keep
the water lettuce rosette
floating. Each leaf is
covered in a layer of
water-repellent hairs,
and is waterproof.
New rosettes
sprout from
stolons that
grow out
sideways.

LAND CREATURES?
When the tide goes out,
the mudskipper stays on the
exposed mudflats of mangrove
swamps. Using its fins for support
and balance, it flips its body
rapidly from side to side, skipping
across the mud.

Water lettuce
Pistia stratiotes

*Finely
branched
roots*

SHOVEL-NOSED CATFISH
Hiding beneath water plants by day,
this fish (right) forages on the riverbed at
night. Three pairs of long sensory barbels help it
to feel its way around. The catfish pokes its long,
flat snout into mud and debris to scavenge for food, as
well as taking live prey such as worms and small fish.

Shovel-nosed catfish
Sorubium lima
(South America)

17

Epiphytes

Up in the rain forest treetops, a special group of plants clothe the branches so thickly that the bark is hidden. These are called epiphytes—plants that live on other plants. They anchor themselves to the stems, trunks, branches, or even leaves of other plants. They do not take either water or food from their hosts. Instead, they use them as a means of reaching the light. After heavy rain, the combined weight of epiphytes and the water they have trapped can be enough to bring down whole branches. In the wettest forests, up to 25 percent of flowering plants and ferns are epiphytes, and there are many more kinds of mosses, liverworts, and lichens. The highest number of epiphytic species are found in Central and South American forests.

PLATYCERIUM
The bracket fronds of this large epiphytic fern loosely clasp the tree trunk, so that a litter of plant debris collects behind it. This compost is moistened by rainwater trickling down the trunk, and a rich humus develops into which the fern grows roots. Hanging clear of the trunk are the fertile, spore-bearing fronds.

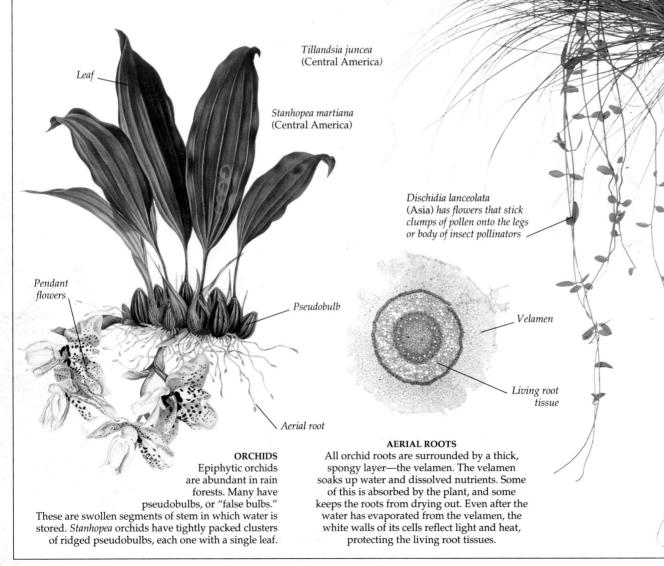

Tillandsia juncea
(Central America)

Stanhopea martiana
(Central America)

Leaf

Pendant flowers

Pseudobulb

Aerial root

Dischidia lanceolata (Asia) *has flowers that stick clumps of pollen onto the legs or body of insect pollinators*

Velamen

Living root tissue

ORCHIDS
Epiphytic orchids are abundant in rain forests. Many have pseudobulbs, or "false bulbs." These are swollen segments of stem in which water is stored. *Stanhopea* orchids have tightly packed clusters of ridged pseudobulbs, each one with a single leaf.

AERIAL ROOTS
All orchid roots are surrounded by a thick, spongy layer—the velamen. The velamen soaks up water and dissolved nutrients. Some of this is absorbed by the plant, and some keeps the roots from drying out. Even after the water has evaporated from the velamen, the white walls of its cells reflect light and heat, protecting the living root tissues.

Anthurium salviniae
(Central America)

*This plant has leaves
that channel rain, dew, and
debris down to a mat of roots*

*This plant absorbs water
from the air through
scales on the leaves*

WATER TANKS

Epiphytic bromeliads, or urn plants, are found in New World rain forests. Each plant has a rosette of stiff leaves around a short stalk. The tightly overlapping leaf bases form a series of cups that collect rainwater. Plant fragments also become trapped, releasing nutrients into the water as they rot. Both water and dissolved minerals are absorbed by the bromeliad through specialized hairs on the leaf surface. These pools support an incredible number of aquatic insects and other creatures. Some frogs even breed in them.

*This plant has silver-
veined leaves that have
a velvety upper surface*

Anthurium crystallinum
(South America)

Aechmea fasciata
(South America)

Branching out

Heavy rain soon drains through the canopy, and the sunshine, though patchy, is very hot. This means that water and dissolved nutrients can be in short supply. Because of this, epiphytes share many of the characteristics of plants that grow in arid (hot and dry) conditions. The leaves have a thick, waxy, waterproof outer layer to reduce evaporation and grow so that rainwater funnels to the roots. The decomposing organic matter caught in water traps provides a source of fertilizer.

Oncidium excavatum
(South America)

Tillandsia usneoides
(Central America)

*Young seedlings
like this have
anchoring roots;
the mature air
plants are a tangle
of stems and
narrow leaves*

Guzmania lingulata
(Central America) *is a
bromeliad that prefers shade*

*Aechmea
purpurea-rosea*
(Brazil)

Climbers

ONE OF THE MOST impressive features of a tropical forest is the abundance of lianas, or climbing plants. Some lianas grow to a huge size, with long stems that climb to the forest canopy in search of light, looping from branch to branch and linking the crowns of trees. Once up in the canopy, they develop branches that bear leaves and flowers. Lianas send feeding roots—also called aerial roots because they dangle in midair—toward ground. When they reach soil, they bury themselves and branch rapidly. These long roots in turn act as supports for other climbing plants.

BLACK SPIDER MONKEY
Spider monkeys spend all their time in the trees, using their long limbs and tail to grip the branches.

ROOT CLIMBERS
These climbers cling to a tree's bark with short clasping roots that come out at right angles from the nodes all along the stem. They either press into the crevices of rough bark or grow around a smooth surface. As the plant gets larger, feeding roots also sprout from the nodes. These roots go straight down to the ground.

Rhaphidophora decursiva

Node

TENDRIL CLIMBERS
Vines like this *Teratostigma* send out straight tendrils that bend away from the light, sweeping slowly around until they come into contact with a stem or leaf. This contact causes the tendril to coil tightly and quickly—it wraps itself around a supporting stem within a few minutes.

Teratostigma
(Southeast Asia)

Rhaphidophora decursiva
(Southeast Asia)

Aerial root

The fig sends aerial roots to the ground, where they spread through the soil

Mesh

Roots grow branches that form a woody mesh around the trunk of the host

Fig

Fig kills the host tree by strangulation and by blocking out its light

STRANGLERS
Strangler figs destroy host trees when they grow. They begin life as epiphytes, and become very tall trees with hollow trunks.

Begonia serratipetala

GROWING TOGETHER
Strong climbing plants such as *Rhaphidophora decursiva* have juvenile leaves very different from the adult foliage. The young plants have short stems, with closely overlapping "shingle" leaves that press against the bark to prevent loss of water. Later, long-stalked adult leaves develop. In contrast, the climbing *Begonia serratipetala* is delicate, and its leaves shrivel if exposed to dry air.

REACHING THE TOP
Tall rain forest trees are draped with the leafless stems and aerial roots of climbers. These need to be strong but flexible, so that they do not snap when the trees that support them sway in high winds.

Vine
Mondia whitei

TWINING PLANTS
These plants reach the light with stems that twine around a support. Once one stem is secured, others from the same plant twine around it so that a tough, twisted cord is made.

Fern scrambling toward light over moss

Downward-curving stamens

Leptochilus decurrens (Southeast Asia)

Young frond

The internode, or bare stem between nodes, gets longer as the plant grows

Flower bud

CLIMBING FERNS
Ferns such as *Leptochilus decurrens* start life on the damp, shady forest floor. The young fronds are thin and delicate. The older ones are much tougher, with a thick, waxy surface. These climbers reach the light by scrambling over other vegetation.

PASSIFLORA
There are about 400 species of *Passiflora* in tropical jungles, most of them in tropical America. The young plant has short stems and no tendrils. It may stay this way for months on the shady forest floor. If a gap appears in the canopy overhead, the plant begins to grow rapidly up toward the light.

Three-lobed leaf

Passiflora (South America)

Central American jungles

ONCE THE CENTERS of the great Maya and Aztec civilizations, the small countries bridging North and South America contain an incredible diversity of plant and animal life. A large number of plants native to the region are found nowhere else, and it is home to many important tropical crops, including pawpaws, allspice, and vanilla. Central America and the Caribbean islands are particularly rich in bird life. The small country of Panama has more bird species than are found in the whole of North America, including migratory species that overwinter in the warm rain forests, before returning to North America to breed.

ANCIENT CULTURE
The Maya civilization flourished in Belize and Guatemala until A.D. 800. Mayans left many examples of intricately decorated pottery showing how they admired animals, such as this jaguar.

Epiphytic orchid
Stanhopea wardii

CARIBBEAN ISLANDS

Caribbean Sea

CENTRAL AMERICA

Sharp, poisonous spines to protect caterpillar from predators

□ *Former rain forest*
■ *Actual rain forest*

CENTRAL AMERICA
Before the 16th century, the Caribbean islands were almost completely covered with rain forest. Nearly all of this was cleared, island after island, to make way for sugar plantations. The rain forests of mainland Central America now cover about 40 percent of their original areas; only Belize still has as much as 60 percent.

Postman butterfly caterpillar
Heliconius melpomene

JUNGLE COLOR
Different kinds of *Heliconia* grow in shady conditions beside streams or in overgrown clearings. The striking flowerheads are made up of brightly colored bracts, each one enclosing a number of small flowers.

WELL NOURISHED

These butterflies are able to live for six to nine months because they feed on protein-rich pollen as well as nectar. They squirt enzymes onto the pollen, which turns it into a "soup" that can be sucked up. Their longer lifespan means that they can lay more eggs.

Winged central column

Postman butterfly
Heliconius melpomene

BRIEF BEAUTY

Hanging in fragrant sprays, the large waxy flowers of this lowland epiphytic orchid are short-lived, withering after pollination. Each flower has a winged central column with fleshy lips, designed to attach the clumps of pollen firmly to its pollinator, the euglossine bee.

Scarlet macaw
Ara macao

WINGS IN THE TREETOPS

Raucous calls reveal the presence of these macaws in the treetops. These brightly colored, social birds squabble over nesting sites – tree holes at least 100 ft (30 m) above the ground. Their diet consists mostly of seeds, many of which are protected by a hard shell. The macaw uses its tongue to position a seed in the upper part of its beak, then cracks it with the lower part – just like a pair of pincers.

PROGRAMMED TO EAT

The postman butterfly caterpillar eats enormous numbers of leaves in the short time before it metamorphoses into a butterfly. Many postman butterfly caterpillars feed on *Passiflora* (passion flower) vines. For egg-laying purposes, the female butterfly always selects young shoots or tendrils that do not already have eggs on them, as the first caterpillars to hatch will devour any younger ones.

JUNGLE GOLD

The golden beetle *Plusiotis resplendens* is about 1 in (3 cm) long and is found only in Costa Rica. The adult beetles eat leaves, but the larvae feed on soft, rotting plants.

Slipper orchid
Paphiopedilum callosum
(Southeast Asia)

Sweet success

A FLOWER HAS TO BE POLLINATED before seeds can develop. Flowers are made up of petals around the male (stamens) and female (carpels) reproductive parts that produce its seeds. During pollination, pollen is transferred from the stamens to the stigma at the tip of a carpel. Pollination almost always takes place between plants of the same species, and stamens and carpels are often arranged so that self-pollination is not possible. Most jungle plants are pollinated by insects, birds, or other small animals. In order to attract their pollinators, flowers offer sugary nectar or protein-rich pollen as food. They draw attention to themselves with brightly colored petals or strong scents.

Line acting as nectar guide

Pouched petal

Short-tailed leaf-nose bat carrying baby
Anoura geoffroyi
(South America)

EXOTIC ORCHID
Tropical slipper orchids are often pollinated by a single species of bee or hoverfly. The insect is guided to the center of the flower, where it is slippery, so it falls into a pouched petal. The only way out is to climb up hairs at the back of the pouch, a route that takes it past the stamens and pollen sacs.

BAT POLLINATION
Bat-pollinated flowers such as *Pachira aquatica* open at dusk, just as the bats are waking up. The bats are attracted to the flowers by a sour smell, and the flowers are arranged so that bats can reach them easily. As a bat drinks the nectar, its furry head is dusted with pollen from the long stamens, which it carries to the female stigma of the next flower.

Long stamens

NECTAR SIPPER
Bats that feed exclusively on nectar have long tongues with a brushlike tip, which quickly mops up pollen as well as droplets of nectar. These bats can hover while feeding.

Shaving-brush tree
Pachira aquatica
(South America)

THE LONG AND THE SHORT OF IT

Most flowers are insect-pollinated. Short-tongued bees, flies, and beetles pollinate flat or cup-shaped flowers as they gather pollen and nectar. Only insects with longer tongues can reach nectar hidden in tubular flowers. This flowering shrub (*Steriphoma pardoxum*) has long stamens that ripen before the stigma, in order to prevent self-pollination. It is pollinated by long-tongued insects such as hawkmoths.

Orchid bee
Euglossa assarophora
(South America)

EUGLOSSINE BEES

Male euglossine bees, known as orchid bees, pollinate orchids when they visit them, scraping aromatic (strong-smelling) substances from parts of the flower. Females forage over a large area, pollinating a wide variety of plants at all levels of the forest.

Orchid bee
Euglossa intersecta
(South America)

PARALLEL EVOLUTION

Sunbirds are the Old World equivalents of the hummingbirds of the Western Hemisphere. Like them, they feed on nectar from flowers, and they eat many insects as well. But sunbirds do not hover – they perch beside the flowers.

Scarlet-chested sunbird
Nectarinia senegalensis
(Africa)

Steriphoma pardoxum
(South America)

Wings flap at least 90 times per second

Brown violet-ear
Colibri delphinea
(Central America)

QUICK AS A FLASH

Hummingbirds hover in front of flowers, their wings making a figure-eight movement, which allows them to maneuver easily. Bird-pollinated flowers are usually red or bright orange. Nectar, though sweet and sugary, is low in protein content, so nectar-eating birds need a constant supply of flowers to get enough to eat. The pollen eaten with the nectar is a valuable source of protein.

Hummingbird sucks up nectar with the long tongue inside its beak

Hotlips
Cephaelis elata
(Central America)

Seed dispersal

Pₗₐₙₜₛ ɴᴇᴇᴅ to spread their seeds so that they have room to grow. Because they cannot move around, they rely on wind, animals, water, or explosive pods to scatter their seeds. The fruit wall is part of this scattering mechanism. Some fruits are winged or cottony to help the seeds become airborne. Some are air-filled and float on water. More familiar are the juicy, brightly colored fruits that spread their seeds by enticing animals, including people, to eat their succulent flesh. These seeds are spread when animals spit them out, let them fall, or pass them out in droppings deposited some distance away.

RATTAN PALMS
Rattan palms produce clusters of fruits. These usually contain a single seed enveloped in a fleshy layer that is eaten by birds and animals. As hard-shelled seeds pass through the digestive tract of an animal, their outer wall is eaten away by digestive juices. This makes water absorption and germination easier.

Fruit is in clusters at base of frond

Rattan seeds
Calamus paspalanthus
(Southeast Asia)

Hard seed case

ATTRACTIVE MORSEL
This *Elaeocarpus angustifolia* seed was enclosed in a purple fruit with oily flesh. The fruit is swallowed whole by birds, such as hornbills.

BURIED AND FORGOTTEN
Inside the fibrous case of *Loxococcus rupicola* is a hard nutty seed that is dispersed by rodents. These gnawing animals bury seeds for future feasts. Forgotten caches germinate and grow.

Red lemur palm fruit
Lemurophoenix halleuxii
(Madagascar)

A CASE THAT IS HARD TO CRACK?
Larger animals and fruit-eating bats often carry fruit to a safe place before eating it. Some seeds are then spat out or discarded, especially if they are too hard to crack.

Pigafetta filaris
(Australasia)

FRUIT EATER
This lemur lives in tall trees beside rivers in southern Madagascar. Fruit is the most important part of its diet, although it also eats insects and leaves.

Hard, nutty seed

Ring-tailed lemur
Lemur catta
(Madagascar)

Sago palm
Metroxylon sagu
(Australasia)

SCALY FRUIT
Pigafetta, sago, and rattan palms are closely related species with fruits enclosed in shiny, overlapping scales. Beneath a sago palm's scales is a corky layer that enables the fruit to float, thus dispersing its single seed. A sago palm dies after it has fruited.

Epauletted
fruit bat
*Epomophorus
wahlbergi* (Africa)

Kapok
seed

Kapok pod
Ceiba pentandra

BLOWING IN THE WIND
Towering above the forest
canopy, the kapok tree
employs the wind to
disperse its seeds. Each
fruit pod is up to 7 in
(18 cm) long. As it
ripens, the pod wall
dries and eventually
splits, releasing a
mass of shiny floss
in which the seeds
are embedded. As
this is blown far
and wide by the
winds, the seeds
will fall out.

FRUITFUL FIGS
Figs are found in all tropical
rain forests. They are a significant
part of the diet of many animals,
including birds, bats, and monkeys. To keep the small
fig seeds from being destroyed by digestive juices, the
fig flesh contains a laxative that ensures that the seeds
pass through an animal's body quickly.

*Pod burst open
to disperse seeds*

Nypa palm seed
Nypa fruticans
(Southeast Asia)

*Fibrous
wall*

SEEDS AFLOAT
Seeds that are
spread by water need
a waterproof layer
to prevent them from
becoming waterlogged.
They also need an air-
filled fruit wall to keep them
afloat. Nypa palms grow in the
brackish (salty) mud of mangrove
swamps. Their fruits have a thick
fibrous wall that enables them to float
for several months, during which time
the seed inside may start to germinate.

Dusk to dawn

NIGHT COMES SWIFTLY in the tropics, where there are no lingering hours of twilight. As the sun sinks toward the horizon, daytime creatures return to their roosts or nests, and a new group of animals awakens. Because some animals are active by day and others by night, different species of animals that would otherwise compete for food and space are separated. The cooler night air brings out insects and amphibians with thin, moist skins, and small mammals that hunt on the forest floor. Nocturnal (nighttime) animals are specially adapted—many have huge eyes or acutely sensitive ears and noses. Yet the jungle is never completely dark. The moon shines on clear nights. Fireflies flash through the trees, and phosphorescent fungi glow eerily on the forest floor, until they are devoured by beetles.

NIGHT FEEDER
By day, Franquet's epauleted bats roost in small groups, hanging from thin branches usually 13-20 ft (4-6 m) above the ground. As night falls, they fly off to feed on fruit, large numbers often gathering in a heavily laden tree. Fruit bats have large eyes with good vision, but they locate ripe fruit with their keen sense of smell.

Franquet's epauleted bat
Epomops franqueti
(Africa)

Wings folded when roosting

FLYING HOME TO ROOST
Just before darkness falls, parties of toucans fly off to roost in selected trees. They look ungainly in flight, but although large, their colorful bills are very light in weight. As dawn breaks, the flock once more takes to the air in search of ripe fruit.

Large curved beak for picking and eating fruit

Cuvier's toucan
Rhamphastos cuvieri
(South America)

NIGHT-LIGHTS
Fireflies are not the only insects that glow. Males of this species of click beetle, *Pyrophorus*, from tropical America, fly among the trees flashing in special sequences that are answered only by females of the same species.

NECTAR-SIPPERS

Night-flying moths feed on the nectar of sweetly scented, pale-colored flowers, many of which are open only for a single night. This African moon moth is one of the largest species, with a wingspan of 5 in (12 cm). The feathery antennae of the male are so sensitive that they can pick up the slightest trace of pheromones (sex hormones) wafting from a female moth.

African moon moth
Argema mimosae
(Africa)

BIG EYES

The vertical pupils of the red-eyed tree frog *Agalychnis callidryas* open up at night to help it see in the very low light levels. By day, the pupils become slits. These frogs live and feed up in the canopy. Only the female comes down to absorb water from a stream before she lays her eggs.

DAWN CHORUS

Just before dawn breaks, howler monkeys set up a noisy chorus. The deafening howls can be heard up to 2 miles (3 km) away, and are produced by air passing over the hyoid bone in the large larynx. Mature males, such as this one, make the loudest howl. The howl can be amplified by their body position. This early morning symphony is a warning to other groups of howlers not to come too close to them and their food supply.

Large eyes for
night vision

Red howler monkey
Alouatta seniculus
(South America)

NIGHT MONKEY

The douroucouli, or night monkey, is the only nocturnal monkey in the world. As night falls, douroucoulis emerge from tree holes to feed on fruit, leaves, insects, and other small animals. Their large, forward-pointing eyes are typical of nocturnal primates, and help them to see in the near-darkness as they climb and leap from branch to branch.

Douroucouli
Aotus trivirgatus
(South America)

DIGGING DOWN

The scaly Indian pangolin, *Manis crassicaudata*, digs a burrow in which it spends the day, emerging at night to forage on the forest floor. Though its sight is weak, it has an acute sense of smell, which it uses to locate ant and termite mounds. Breaking in with the long powerful claws on its forelimbs, the pangolin flicks its very long sticky tongue into chambers full of insects, eggs, and pupae. It is toothless, so the swallowed insects are ground up in the lower part of its stomach.

South American jungles

THE AMAZON BASIN covers a vast area, nearly 2.5 million sq miles (6 million sq km), and is covered by the world's largest expanse of tropical rainforest. This jungle supports more species of plants and animals than anywhere else – about one-fifth of the world's bird and flowering plant species, and about one-tenth of all mammal species. No definite figure can be put on the number of different insects, because many have yet to be identified – or even discovered – by scientists. Amerindian tribes have lived in these forests for about 12,000 years, during which time they have built up a detailed and valuable knowledge of the jungle plants, many of which they use in their everyday lives.

Mouth of Amazon River

SOUTH AMERICA

☐ *Former rain forest*
▨ *Actual rain forest*

SOUTH AMERICA
The forests of the northwest were separated from the Amazonian forests 2 million years ago by the formation of the Andes Mountains. A few small patches are all that remain of the once continuous strip of forest along the Atlantic coast of Brazil.

BODY PAINTING
These Yanomamo girls belong to one of 143 tribal groups remaining in Amazonia. Body painting is popular, with paint from plants such as urucu or achiote. The seeds are wiped directly onto the skin or boiled to make a paste. Each tribe has its favorite patterns.

Aphinte
Bixa orellana

A WAXY SURFACE
Growing naturally beside rivers and around the edges of swampy areas, the Brazilian wax palm, *Copernicia prunifera*, is also cultivated in Brazil for the carnauba wax that covers the surface of its leaves. Carnauba is a top quality wax with a high melting point of 161°F (70°C). It is used chiefly in the cosmetic and polish industries. The wax flakes off leaves that have been picked and dried in the sun. Wax taken from the young leaves is known as "prime yellow," and about 1,300 leaves are needed to obtain 2.2 lbs (1 kg) of wax.

ONE OF MANY

The malachite butterfly is just one of more than 2,000 species of butterfly in the Amazonian jungles. They fly during the day, pausing to feed on over-ripe fruit fermenting on the forest floor.

Malachite butterfly
Metamorpha stelenes

GOLD IN THE FOREST

This beautiful golden monkey is found only in Atlantic coastal rain forests. Golden lion tamarins live in mature forest, where they forage for invertebrates, small animals, and fruit 10-30 ft (3-10 m) up in the liana-covered trees. They came near to extinction in the 1960s, because their habitat was being destroyed and hundreds were being exported as pets every year. Since then, captive breeding programs established in the United States and Europe have resulted in the release of golden lion tamarins back into the wild.

Golden lion tamarin
Leontopithecus rosalia

Long tail for balancing

Buriti palm
Mauritia flexuosa

THE TREE OF LIFE

Nothing of this tall palm goes to waste. The Amerindians use it as a source of food, fibers, wood, cork, and thatching. Wine made from its vitamin C-rich fruits is given to the elderly and sick.

NOT SO LAZY

Despite its name, the three-toed sloth *Bradypus tridactylus* is not a lazy animal. It is perfectly adapted to its life up in the canopy. There is little protein in its diet, and to conserve energy it hangs upside down and its strong claws lock so tightly onto branches that it does not fall off even when asleep – or dead!

Amazon lily
Eucharis amazonica

MYSTERIOUS POWERS

The Amazon lily grows on the lower slopes of the Andes. The Kofan tribes of western Colombia and northern Ecuador boil the whole plant, including its bulb, to make a tea. This is drunk by men before they hunt monkeys, in the belief that it will make them more accurate with the blowpipe.

Beside the water

The Riverbank is the domain of animals that live both on land and in water. The vegetation here is particularly dense, since the open expanse of water allows extra light to reach the ground. This mosaic of water, overhanging branches, and tangles of waterside ferns, sedges, and saplings provides an ideal environment for animals that live and breed on land but enter the water to hunt and feed. However, heavy rains sometimes cause a river to overflow its banks, and this puts animals nesting close to the water's edge at risk.

JAWS OF THE RIVERBANK
The saltwater crocodile, *Crocodylus porosus*, is the world's largest crocodile. It can reach 25 ft (7.5 m) in length and weigh as much as 3 tons.

UMBRELLA GRASS
The sedge, *Cyperus alternifolia*, has leaves that radiate from the top of its tall stems like the spokes of an umbrella. Underwater, the roots grow into an impenetrable tangle that helps stabilize the edges of swamps in which it grows.

WARY WATER LIZARD
Water dragons are agamid lizards that live beside water in the forests of Southeast Asia and Australia. Although they are mainly tree-dwellers, they can run quickly over the ground on their two hind legs, usually aiming for the next tree. When not searching for invertebrates, eggs, and nestlings to eat, they spend most of their time resting along a branch overhanging the water. They are extremely wary and, at the slightest disturbance, will drop off into the water, which may be as much as 30 ft (9 m) below.

Crested water dragon
Physignathus sp.
(Asia)

WATERSIDE PLANT
The waterside plant *Thalia geniculata* is abundant in marshes and seasonally flooded ground near rivers. It has large waxy leaves and spreads by means of tuberous roots.

An alert crested water dragon stands on all four feet, watching for danger

32

GIANT OTTER
Each family group of giant otters has its own territory. Ungainly on land, these creatures are excellent swimmers—they use their large, webbed feet as paddles and their muscular tail as a rudder. When they catch a fish, they carry it to the surface to eat.

FROGS IN DANGER
Originally inhabitants of Madagascan rain forests, these endangered tomato frogs, *Dyscophus autongili*, are now adapting to other habitats, as the forests dwindle in size.

Eyes on long stalks watch for danger; rest of body is camouflaged

Fiddler crab
Uca vocans

SWAMP DWELLER
The fiddler crab makes its burrow in the thick mud of mangrove swamps, emerging when the tide goes out. Only the males have a single, much enlarged front pincer. Useless for gathering food, it is used to signal alluringly to female crabs, and also to wrestle with rival males.

Bat has a wingspan of 24 in (60 cm)

FISHING FOR FOOD
The bulldog, or fisherman, bat, *Noctilio leporinus*, skims low over still water, using echolocation to detect ripples. It uses its sharply hooked claws to gaff fish out of the water. Its prey is either eaten on the wing or carried to a nearby roost.

Long tail for balance and to use as a rudder in water

Dry, scaly skin that is regularly shed, or sloughed off, to reveal a new layer

Powerful sharp-clawed feet for climbing

CURARE

The rough bark or roots of some *Strychnos* vines are ingredients of curare, used as an arrow poison by some tribes. In the past, each tribe had its own closely guarded secret recipe for making the poison.

Solid lump of prepared curare

Hidden dangers

LURKING IN THE DEPTHS of the jungle are animals and plants equipped with a lethal battery of foul-tasting poisons. They either manufacture the poisons themselves, or use those that were in their food, advertising their hidden armory with their bright colors. Venomous creatures such as snakes and spiders need powerful toxins to subdue prey that might inflict injury during a struggle. Plants contain poisons to prevent herbivores from eating all their foliage. The only indications that their green leaves are unpleasant are the smell and taste. They can afford to lose a few leaves, and animals soon learn to avoid them.

TAKING AIM
This Penan hunter in Borneo uses darts tipped with poisons. The poisons kill the catch quickly, so that it falls close to the hunter.

POTTED POISON
After the ingredients for curare are pounded together, the mixture is boiled or mixed with cold water. The thick liquid is strained off and kept in hollow gourds.

Arrow tipped with coating of curare

Living with poisons

The poisonous nature of animals and plants are understood by the peoples who live in the jungle. Many highly toxic plants are used in everyday life, both for hunting and, in far smaller doses, as medicines. Arrows are tipped with concoctions of plant or animal poisons. Poisonous leaves or sap are used to contaminate stretches of water so that many fish die at the same time. The poisons are mostly inactive if taken by mouth, so the meat is safe to eat.

Arrows used to hunt monkeys and other mammals

SAFETY TIPS
South American hunters tie their arrows together with cord and keep them securely in a bamboo quiver for safety. They have to be careful that they do not accidentally prick themselves with a poisoned tip.

Bamboo quiver

IMMUNE TO DANGER
A female postman butterfly lays her eggs on the youngest *Passiflora* leaves, because they contain the least poison. The larvae absorb the poisons into their bodies.

Small postman butterfly
Heliconius erato
(South America)

Blue poison dart frog
Dendrobates azureus
(South America)

POISON DART FROG
This forest-floor frog exudes powerful poisons from all over its skin if anything bothers it. Amerindian hunters use the poison to coat their blowpipe darts.

POISONOUS PLANT
If a plant loses most or all of its leaves, its ability to take in carbon dioxide and manufacture sugars is greatly reduced. The foliage of this large *Passiflora* climber contains a complex cocktail of chemicals, including bitter-tasting alkaloids and compounds that contain cyanide. Mammals will not eat it, and only a few leaf-eating insects such as postman butterflies and some species of beetle have evolved ways of overcoming its toxicity.

Thai monocled cobra
Naja kaouthia
(South-Eastasia)

Eyes set at side of head

Characteristic hood

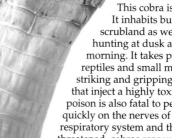

Giant tiger centipede
Scolopendra gigantea
(Africa)

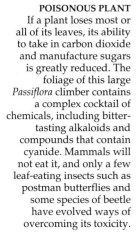

FATAL FEET
Dramatic orange and black stripes warn of this centipede's toxicity. It injects its prey with poisonous venom, using the first pair of its many legs, which have sharply tipped claws.

SUDDEN DEATH
This cobra is greatly feared. It inhabits buildings and scrubland as well as dense jungle, hunting at dusk and in the early morning. It takes prey, such as other reptiles and small mammals, by striking and gripping with front fangs that inject a highly toxic venom. The poison is also fatal to people, acting quickly on the nerves of the human respiratory system and the heart. When threatened, cobras rear up, hiss, and expand their "hood" by raising the elongated ribs of the neck region.

Nature's architects

THE RAIN FOREST PROVIDES tree holes, tangles of lianas, and plenty of other hideaways. In spite of this, numerous creatures build custom-made homes from forest materials. Social insects such as bees, wasps, ants, and termites construct elaborate nests inside of which a teeming mass of insects live and tend their larvae. These large colonies need well-protected structures to keep predators out. Some structures last for years. Birds are master weavers, but their nests are used only to rear young. Even less permanent are the beds made by gorillas. Every night, they prepare a mattress of leaves on the ground or among low branches.

THE CUTTING EDGE
Leafcutter ants (*Atta* sp.) live in underground nests in colonies of up to five million. "Media" workers only 10 mm long travel up into the canopy, where they snip out neat pieces of leaves with their jaws. A continuous trail of ants carries these like flags back to the nest. There, 2-mm-long "minima" workers chew the leaves to a paste, mixing it with feces. This concoction is used to grow a fungus on which the ants feed.

Ant domatia
Myrmecodia tuberosa

Scar left by fallen leaf

Stem is not lived in by ants

Thick fibrous stem

CLOSE PARTNERSHIP
The relationship between *Iridomyrmex* ants and the epiphyte *Myrmecodia tuberosa* is just one of many fascinating jungle partnerships. The ants enter air spaces inside the plant through tiny holes in the plant wall. They establish their colony, rearing young and setting up fungus gardens. Fragments of dead plants and animals are brought in to nourish the fungus. The decaying matter then provides valuable internal compost for the host plant.

BAT CAMP
A few species of New World spear-nosed bats make their own daytime shelters from large leaves such as palm fronds and *Heliconia* foliage. They either bite a neat line across the veins of fan-shaped leaves, or along the midrib of long leaves, so that part of the leaf blade flops down. During the day, the bats roost in their green tents. Males are usually solitary, but females, such as these Honduran white bats (*Ectophylla alba*), cluster in small groups, especially while rearing their young.

Airholes where ants enter

Swollen base of plant

Atta ants carrying
leaves back to nest

Paper wasps
Polistes sp.
(Central America)

*Adult emerging
from cell*

BOWER BUILDER
Male satin bowerbirds (*Ptilonorhynchus
violaceus*) build their bowers on the
forest floor to attract mates. They make
them in low-growing vegetation, and
arrange colored feathers, fruits, and
flowers in the bower to tempt the
female. Different species of bowerbirds
often favor particular colors.

Female worker

*Umbrella-like
cap to keep
out the rain*

MUD HOME
Termites play an important role in
the decomposition of dead trees,
fallen logs, and other plant debris.
They either feed directly on this
material or carry it back to their
nests, where, like the leafcutter
ants, they grow a special fungus on it
in carefully tended gardens. Termites
that nest underground build columns or
mounds above ground level to create an
air flow through the nest. This *Cubitermes*
column is made of sticky pellets of soil
mixed with saliva that harden when dry.

Egg

Queen termite
lays one egg every
three seconds

PAPER NEST MAKERS
Paper wasps build combs of hexagonal
cells. The comb does not have an outer
wall and the "paper" is wood pulp that
has been chewed to a paste. A single
female mates and starts the nest, making a
cluster of small cells that she attaches to a
low branch by a stalk. She lays a single egg
in each cell. The cells are lengthened to
keep pace with the growing grub. After the
grub pupates, female workers take over
the care of the larvae. The newest cells of
the comb are always at the bottom,
although older cells are often reused.

DEADLY WEAPONS
Tribes make their hunting
weapons from rain forest
materials. This spear
from Guyana is made
from feathers, wood,
bone, and basketry.
The palmwood bow is
strung with rattan,
and the three-tipped
fish arrow is made
of wood, bamboo,
reed, and cane.

House and home

WHEN PEOPLE NEED shelter, there
is no shortage of building materials
in the jungle. Slender tree trunks are
felled for use as walls; palm fronds are
cut for thatching; and tough cording
is prepared from lianas. Some tribes
build separate family homes grouped
together in a forest clearing. Others
favor one enormous structure that
houses the whole community, and
inside of which each family has its
own hearth. Styles vary, but the houses
share some features, such as an
overhanging thatched roof to keep out
the rain. Inside, each dwelling contains
everyday utensils and weapons,
skillfully made from natural materials
such as bamboo and cane.

POTTER'S ART
The neolithic Kintampo culture brought
pottery to the African rain forests.
Containers such as this partly glazed pot
from lower Zaire are still made today.

*String made
of rattan*

*Bow made
of palm*

Model of a rain forest
house without walls
(South America)

WELL SHIELDED
Warring tribespeople held
shields to ward off blows
from spears or arrows.
Today, they are more often
used for ceremonial
purposes. This colorful shield
from Borneo is decorated on
the front with human hair.
The reverse depicts tigers and
dragons, symbols of strength
and invincibility.

*Sturdy tree
trunks form
basic structure*

Human hairs

Palmwood bow
and fish arrow
(Papua New Guinea)

Dyak shield
(Borneo)

HIGH AND DRY

This hill tribe house in northern Thailand has central living quarters. It is well screened from the rain by thatching that sweeps down on all sides. The house is set on poles above the ground to keep the floor dry. Outside, there is plenty of shelter beneath the roof for outdoor tasks.

NATIVE HOUSE AT DORERI

Traveling by water is the easiest way to get around much of New Guinea because of the dense jungle vegetation. Many settlements are therefore built on the riverside or by the coast. This large house has been built on stilts over the water, probably in order to escape destructive insects such as termites.

LIVING IN THE RAIN FOREST

This model gives some idea of the the furniture and utensils found in a native rain forest house in South America. The occupants sleep in hammocks, knotted from cords. They weave lightweight vessels from cane or palm leaves, but heavy duty containers are made with strips of wood. Canoe paddles and weapons are also shaped from wood, and all of these items are stored by hanging them on the walls of the house. Clay pots are not made by all tribes, but are often acquired by trading.

Hammock

Fishing basket

CHIEF'S YAM HOUSE

Yams are an important staple food. On the Trobriand Islands, off the coast of New Guinea, yams are also a central part of complicated rituals that maintain goodwill and kinship between clans related by marriage. After the yam harvest, the chief's yam house is filled first. This brightly decorated house is thatched and has well-ventilated walls. This allows air to circulate so that the yams do not get moldy.

African jungles

OIL PALM
This 33-65 ft (10-20 m) palm (*Elaeis guineensis*) yields two valuable oils – palm oil from the red fibrous fruit pulp and palm kernel oil from the seeds.

Aʟᴛʜᴏᴜɢʜ ᴛʜᴇʏ ᴄᴏɴᴛᴀɪɴ an impressive 17,000 species of flowering plants, African rain forests have fewer species than those of either America or Asia. There are also fewer kinds of ferns. This is because the climate of Africa became much drier during the last ice age, which ended about 12,000 years ago. Many animals, insects, and plants died out during this period. Those that survived lived in three well-separated pockets of forest that remained moist. As the ice retreated from the lands farther north, the climate became wetter, and the surviving rain forest species spread out from their isolated refuges.

STICKY FEET
The Madagascan day gecko (*Phelsuma madagascariensis*) has Velcro-like toe pads so it can cling to branches – and even run along their undersides.

☐ *Former rain forest*
☐ *Actual rain forest*

AFRICA

AFRICA
More than 80 percent of Africa's rain forest is in the central region. Along the coast of West Africa, the remaining forests are in fragmented pockets, but some countries are setting up conservation zones.

Madagascar

FLOWERS IN THE CANOPY
Of all the epiphytic flowering plants and ferns that grow in African jungles, over 60% are different kinds of orchids, and little is known about their life histories. *Polystachya galeata* comes from Sierra Leone, where new reserves will help to safeguard its future and that of other vulnerable species.

FAST GROWTH
Hibiscus shrubs grow quickly, up to 7 ft (2 m) tall. They flourish along the edges of the forest, where there is the most light. Their large flowers attract pollinators such as bees and butterflies.

Hibiscus
Hibiscus calyphyllus

GOOD APPETITES
African elephants prefer to browse the dense vegetation of clearings and forest margins. Over half of their diet is foliage from trees and large climbers, but they will travel far into the depths of the jungle to find their favorite tree fruits.

Black-and-white colobus
Colobus guereza
(Africa)

Senegal parrot
Poicephalus senegalensis
(Africa)

FLASH OF COLOR
The green and gold Senegal parrots migrate across savanna grassland into the forest to take advantage of ripening crops of fruits and seeds. They nest in unlined tree holes.

FAMILY GROUP
The guereza is one of four kinds of black-and-white colobus monkey that live in family groups in the treetops. It is found in central and eastern Africa. Because these monkeys eat a wide range of readily available leaves, they do not need a very large home range.

Only males have a silver back

Large, powerful hands

HEAD OF THE TRIBE
This silverback lowland gorilla (*Gorilla gorilla gorilla*) is a mature male. He is the dominant head of a social group that also contains mature females and young gorillas. Silverbacks are gentle with their young, but as the males reach maturity, they have to leave the troop and form their own social group. Gorillas travel slowly through the forest, resting, playing, and eating leaves, stems, and shoots.

Wing-stalked yam powder

Medicines

MOST OF THESE PLANTS are very poisonous. Yet, if taken at the right dosage, they help save lives or alleviate suffering. A rain forest can be compared to a giant pharmacy where tribespeople find remedies for all their ills. Only some of the medicinal plants have been screened scientifically. It is important to do this either before the plants become extinct, or the tribes, with their accumulated knowledge, disappear. Many plants are known to contain beneficial compounds. Others have a more spiritual importance. Some tribespeople think if a plant looks like a bodily organ, it will cure that organ of all ailments.

Wing-stalked yam
Dioscorea alata
(Southeast Asia)

INDIAN YAM
Yams are a good source of diosgenin, a compound used in oral contraceptives. It is also used in treatments for rheumatoid arthritis and rheumatic fever.

SKIN MEDICINE
Chaulmoogra ointment is an Indian preparation rubbed onto the skin to treat leprosy and skin infections.

Seed oil used in chaulmoogra ointment

Hydnocarpus fruit and seeds
Hydnocarpus kurzii
(Southeast Asia)

Red cinchona bark
Cinchona succirubra
(South America)

Dried tongue of pirarucu fish
(South America)

Quinine stored in the bark

Guarana bark
Paullinia cupana
(South America)

HARD MEDICINE
This hard fruit comes from the *Hydnocarpus* tree, grown in Burma, Thailand, and India for its medicinal properties.

PRECIOUS PLANT
The red cinchona tree is one of four commercial kinds of *Cinchona*. The quinine extracted from the bark and roots is an important part of the treatment of malaria, although synthetic drugs are also available today.

Heckel chew stick
Garcinia kola
(Africa)

STIMULATING DRINKS
Guarana plants contain caffeine and are made into tonic drinks all over South America. Tribes grate the seeds (above) or bark into water with the rough, dried tongue of the pirarucu fish. Strong bitter doses are used to get rid of intestinal worms. The seeds are used commercially in carbonated drinks.

Rosy periwinkle
Catharanthus rosea
(Africa)

Carved handle of chew stick

Entire seed

Seed with seed coat removed

A ROSY FUTURE
This one small plant gave hope to cancer sufferers when compounds were isolated from its leaves in the 1950s. Two alkaloids taken from its leaves – vincristine and vinblastine – are now used particularly in the treatment of Hodgkin's disease and childhood leukemia.

CHEW IT AND SEE
For centuries, in parts of Africa, tribespeople have used chew sticks to keep their teeth clean. Woods such as *Garcinia* and the toothbrush tree (*Salvadora persica*) release juices when chewed. These juices appear to act against bacteria in the mouth, cleaning teeth and preventing infection.

Moreton Bay chestnut
Castanospermum australe
(Australasia)

Seed pod of ouabain
Strophanthus hispidus
(Africa)

TAKING HEART
Ouabain was once used by African tribes as an arrow poison. Today, strophanthidin and sarmentogenin are extracted from the seeds of this plant. Strophanthidin is used to treat heart conditions. Sarmentogenin is used to treat rheumatoid arthritis.

Seeds are wind-dispersed

Seeds

Inside of seed case

Calabar bean
Physostigma venenosum
(Africa)

Outside of seed case

Seed kernel

Seed pod

KILL OR CURE?
The exceedingly poisonous seeds of the calabar bean were also known as ordeal beans, because they were used by Africans to decide the guilt of a person. If the eater survived, he or she was innocent. Extracts from the seeds are now used to treat glaucoma (a form of blindness) and high blood pressure.

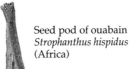

MEDICAL ADVANCES?
The Aborigines used to soak the seeds of the Moreton Bay chestnut for a long time to make them edible. They were washing out the poison castanospermine. Research in the 1980s showed that this substance has significant effects on some viruses including HIV, which causes AIDS.

Forest apes

THE TROPICAL RAIN FORESTS are home to all of the world's apes, and most of its monkeys, although there are no primates in New Guinea and Australia. Many species are able to live close together because they inhabit different levels in the forest canopy, or eat different food. Even so, some groups are highly territorial: one of the lasting impressions of the jungle is the hollering and screeching of monkeys and apes defending their feeding area.

Very long arms

Siamang
Hylobates syndactylus
(Southeast Asia)

Jungle swinger

Gibbons like this siamang use their arms to swing from branch to branch. This process, called brachiation, is an effective way of moving very quickly through the forest canopy and is their usual means of locomotion. They do fall sometimes, with fatal results, but it is the most efficient way of finding the trees that have ripe fruit to eat. Although gibbons use brachiation most, chimpanzees and some monkeys also use this method.

Opposable big toe

GOING FOR A WALK
A gorilla moves around the forest floor on the flat of its feet and its knuckles in quest of the vast quantities of vegetation that it needs to eat every day. Although usually slow-moving, it is capable of bursts of speed when necessary, for example when chasing off a rival.

Gorilla
Gorilla gorilla
(Africa)

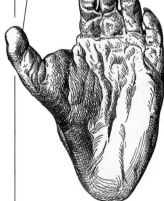

Gorillas have broad feet; the big toes are opposable so they can curl around to grip

Chimpanzees walk and climb in lower canopy, using both hands and feet

Gibbons spend all their time up in trees; they have narrow feet

JUNGLE CHORUS
The siamang is the largest of the gibbons. Each pair lives in the treetops with their offspring. They guard their territory and its vital food supply from neighboring siamangs with a morning and afternoon duet of ear-splitting shrieks and barks. The calls, which can be heard up to 0.6 miles (1 km) away, are given extra resonance by their inflated throat sacs.

Long, narrow hands with thumb cleft almost to the wrist

Forearm that can rotate 180°

Shoulder joint will rotate 360°

Powerful shoulder muscles

Leg outstretched to maximize forward movement

Broad chest

Legs curled up to increase upward stroke of swing

Legs shorter than arms

Long and opposable big toe

CLEVER CHIMP
This primate is very good with its hands. Most chimpanzees use twigs to get tasty morsels from difficult places, but some crack open nuts with stones or branches. They carry their "hammers" for long distances.

Chimpanzee
Pan troglodytes
(Africa)

Mandrill
Mandrillus sphinx
(Africa)

Humboldt's monkey
Lagothrix lagotricha
(South America)

MONKEY ON THE MARCH
Male mandrills live mostly on the forest floor. Females and their young climb up into low undergrowth.

TAIL GRIP
Tree-dwelling woolly monkeys use their prehensile (grasping) tails to grip slippery branches in the canopy.

Hunters and killers

PREDATORS HAVE TO CATCH and kill other animals if they are to survive. They need to detect their prey before it notices them, to stalk, ambush, or outrun it before it escapes, and disable it before it can do them harm. To do all this, hunters must have keen senses. Daytime hunters often rely on their sharp eyesight to find prey. Nocturnal (nighttime) hunters need other skills – a highly developed sense of hearing or smell, or an ability to detect vibrations made by an approaching animal. Prey animals have their own defenses, such as camouflage, so an unlucky hunter goes hungry.

AMBUSHED!
The solitary leopard *Panthera pardus* hunts by stalking prey or leaping on it from above and killing it with a bite to the neck.

Irritant hairs are kicked into face of assailant

DANGER ON EIGHT LEGS
As well as in dry rocky places, the red-kneed tarantula lives in humid forests. During the day, it stays in its silk-lined burrow. After dark, it emerges to hunt for large insects or small vertebrates. It injects prey with a venom that quickly causes paralysis.

Red-kneed tarantula
Brachypelma smithi
(Central America)

Changeable hawk eagle
Spizaetus cirrhatus
(Southeast Asia)

HUNTER IN THE SKY
The changeable hawk eagle has exceedingly good eyesight so it can focus on an animal or bird on the distant ground. From its vantage point, hidden in the foliage of a tall tree, this young bird of prey swoops down swiftly and silently, snatching up its victim with powerful talons (claws).

Tough scaly skin protects the crocodile from flying hooves of prey

KILLER IN THE WATER
The Nile crocodile, together with the saltwater crocodile, is the largest of the jungle predators. It can reach a record 23 ft (7 m) in length, but even the smaller ones are powerful enough to overcome large animals – and people – that come down to the rivers in which it lives. Lurking unseen in the water, crocodiles are capable of surprising bursts of speed as they lunge forward to grab a drinking animal by the muzzle. They kill by dragging their catch under water until it drowns.

SMALL BUT DEADLY

The Southern fer-de-lance is nocturnal and locates warm-blooded prey with heat-sensitive pits between its eyes and nostrils. When a victim is in range, this viper gapes open its mouth, and two long front fangs swing forward. As the snake strikes, these fangs stab, injecting a lethal venom. Most human deaths from snake bites in South America are due to this species.

Juvenile lures prey with yellow tail

Southern fer-de-lance
Bothrops atrox
(South America)

SQUEEZED TO DEATH

The boa constrictor waits motionless until its prey comes close. The animal's air-borne scent is picked up by the snake's tongue and transferred to the sensitive Jacobson's organs on the roof of its mouth. The snake strikes open-mouthed, gripping its catch with its fangs and coiling around the animal's body. Each time the animal breathes out, the snake tightens its coils a little more, until the prey is suffocated.

Boa constrictor
Boa constrictor
(Central and South America)

Formidable array of sharp teeth that are replaced continuously throughout the crocodile's life

Powerful jaws to swallow large prey

Nile crocodile
Crocodylus niloticus
(Africa)

Strong claws to climb quickly up slippery riverbanks

TOOTH AND CLAW

The tiger *Panthera tigris* is a solitary animal that hunts by day or night. The tiger stalks a victim, pouncing on it with formidably clawed forepaws and killing it with a bite to the neck. A tiger's usual diet is deer, goats, and sometimes large cattle. Some tigers, particularly old or injured animals, will go after anything, including people.

Tropical Asia

THE TERM "JUNGLE" is derived from the Hindi word *jangal*, meaning impenetrable forest and undergrowth. Tropical Asia includes many countries and encompasses an enormous area. Part of this is continental mainland, but stretching southeast of this area are the archipelagoes (island groups) of Indonesia and Malaysia, some large, others tiny. It is a diverse and complex region, with many different peoples and histories. Much of the land is covered with tropical forest, including montane forests and the evergreen and monsoon forests of the lowlands, all of which are rich in plant and animal life. With so much coastline, it's not surprising that most of the world's mangrove swamps are found here.

WORKING WITH PLANTS
Palm trees provide a plentiful raw material for many local industries. This Sarawak girl is splitting palm leaves into strips to be woven into matting or baskets.

Prominent eyes with vertical pupils for seeing in low light

TREE SNAKE
The nocturnal green cat snake (*Boiga cyanea*) lives almost exclusively in trees, often near water. It preys on other arboreal (tree-dwelling) creatures, such as tree frogs and lizards. After paralyzing its prey with venom from fangs at the back of its mouth, the snake swallows it whole.

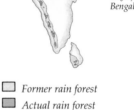

INDIA

Bay of Bengal

China Sea

Malaysia

Indonesia

☐ *Former rain forest*
☐ *Actual rain forest*

Malayan tapir
Tapirus indicus

BROWSER
The tapir is a solitary animal that is most active at night. With its long movable snout, it browses through leaves, fruits, and seeds in the thick jungle growth bordering water.

Strong legs for swimming

INDIA AND SOUTHEAST ASIA
Many generations of human inhabitants have left little of the forest of mainland Southeast Asia in its natural state. Some countries, such as Vietnam, are replanting. Some islands, notably in the Philippines, have lost all their rain forests. Others, such as Borneo, still retain most of their original forest cover, parts of which are still unknown to outsiders.

Rattan palm
Calamus caesius

RATTAN PALMS
There are about 600 species of rattans. These are climbing palms that reach the canopy by means of whips on the tips of the fronds; these whips are covered with hooked spikes. Rattan canes are commercially important for making furniture that is exported all around the world.

Stem can reach over 660 ft (200 m) in length

Shape of petals attracts insects

Leaf sheath covered in hooked spines

ONE OF THE FEW
There are about 70 species of tropical slipper orchid, all of which are found in Southeast Asia. Most of them grow on the ground, but a few grow on trees or rocks. Many slipper orchids are naturally rare because they have specific habitat requirements. Since 1964, 20 new species have been described, and *Paphiopedilum primulinum* itself was only discovered in 1972.

Flower bud

Slipper orchid
Paphiopedilum primulinum

THE GINGER LILY
Many ginger lilies (*Hedychium* spp.) have fragrant, attractive flowers, and their thick underground stems often contain aromatic (nice-smelling) oils. After the tubular flower wilts, a fruit capsule develops. When this is ripe, it splits to reveal three rows of seeds.

Disguise and warning

ANIMALS AND INSECTS use camouflage in an effort to avoid being eaten. Color and shape either make an animal indistinguishable from its background, or trick a predator into thinking that it is dealing with something bigger or more dangerous. Animals with cryptic coloration have colors or patterns that closely match their background. Some patterns seem bold and conspicuous, but they actually make it impossible to see the animal against a mosaic of leaves, twigs, sunshine, and shadow by breaking up the animal's outline. Mimicry takes this kind of camouflage a stage further, in insects that look like leaves, bark, or twigs. The disguise of many insects is so good that, rather than waste time looking for them, flocks of several species of birds will move noisily through the forest like a wave. What small creatures one bird dislodges or disturbs, the bird behind snaps up.

MIMICKING A SNAKE
When disturbed, the caterpillar of the hawkmoth *Leucorhampha ornatus* mimics a small venomous pit viper. It does this by swinging the front part of its body upside down, inflating its thorax to look like a snake's head.

False leaf katydid
Ommatopia pictifolia
(Central America)

STARTLE DISPLAY
The forewings of the false leaf katydid are near-perfect replicas of dead leaves. When motionless, it blends well with low-growing vegetation. However, if it is discovered, this katydid has a second line of defense. In one quick movement, the forewings part to reveal a startling display of eyespots. This display should scare a predator long enough for the katydid to escape.

CHANGING COLOR
The chameleon's colors intensify, with spots and stripes of purple rapidly appearing. His tail straightens, and he takes up a more aggressive stance, puffing up his body to make it look bigger.

Parson's chameleon
Chamaeleo parsonii
(Africa)

REACTION TIME
Contrary to popular belief, a male chameleon does not change colour to match different backgrounds. But at the sight of a rival entering his territory, the response is immediate.

Each eye swivels independently, so the chameleon can look in two directions at the same time

COLOR CHANGE IN CHAMELEONS

The skin of chameleons contains a small range of colored pigments in specialized cells called chromatophores. Those that contain black pigment (melanin) lie deeper in the skin. When facing an intruder, a hormone is released from the pituitary gland. This hormone triggers a surge of melanin pigment to the surface of the skin, and the skin color darkens.

DARKER AND DARKER

His color is now at its most intense. The red eyes and patches of red and green stand out against the deep blackish purple. In an attempt to scare away the intruder, he hisses and lunges forward.

Warning coloration

Some poisonous animals and insects are conspicuously marked with bright colors and striking patterns that warn would-be predators, usually birds, that they taste awful. Often, the strategy is copied by non-poisonous species. It is known as Batesian mimicry, after Henry Walter Bates, the man who first described it. A change of color is also used to communicate with a member of the same species. It can reflect a change of mood, scare off a rival, or signal to a potential mate during the breeding season.

Tiger moth
Ormeticia temporata
(Central America)

ALTERNATIVE DEFENSE

Unlike many other insects, moths and butterflies cannot sting attackers, or defend themselves by biting. Instead, they have other methods. This tiger moth is well protected by its bold warning coloration. The bright yellow stripes on the wings act to discourage or frighten predators.

CAMOUFLAGED CAT

Light-colored fur with dark stripes, spots, or blotches imitates the dappled effect of sunlight in the dense vegetation of the rain forest. It makes an effective camouflage for jungle cats. Tigers rely on their ability to remain unseen as they stalk an intended victim, until they are close enough to pounce.

Tricks and traps

AT ALL LEVELS of the rain forest, there is a host of alert, wary creatures with a strong instinct for survival. A predator always has to outsmart its prey if it is to catch enough to eat. Some hunters combine trickery and deception with patience and the ability to move at lightning speed. Plants have a few tricks of their own. Sap-sucking insects may have their mouthparts gummed up by an unexpected flow of sticky latex. Plants that grow on poor or peaty soils cannot get enough nutrients. In order to survive, some of these plants have turned into carnivores.

Nectar-secreting gland

Leaf blade

Monkey cup
Nepenthes mirabilis

NETTED
Instead of waiting for an insect to fly into its web, the net-casting spider (*Dinopus* spp.) nets its prey. Suspended from lines of silk attached to a twig, it spins a small web. Holding the web with its four front legs, the spider hangs upside down and waits. When an unsuspecting insect comes close, the spider drops the net and captures its prey.

SLIPPERY SLOPE
The rim of the pitcher plant is very slippery. Small vertebrates and insects lose their footing and fall into the trap.

Pitcher develops at tip of leaf

Partly digested insects

Digestive gland

HUNGRY PLANT
Insects are attracted by the color of the pitcher plants and by nectar secreted around the rim. Once the insect falls in, it can't get out. It is digested by enzymes in the water half-filling each pitcher and is absorbed into the plant. The largest pitcher plants have pitchers 30 cm (12 in) long that hold 4 pints (2 liters) of water.

DEADLY LEAVES
The gaboon viper (*Bitis gabonica*) is patterned just like the sun-flecked leaves on the forest floor. It remains motionless and invisible until a small mammal or bird strays too close. Its 2-in-long (5 cm-) fangs inject a venom that is almost instantly fatal.

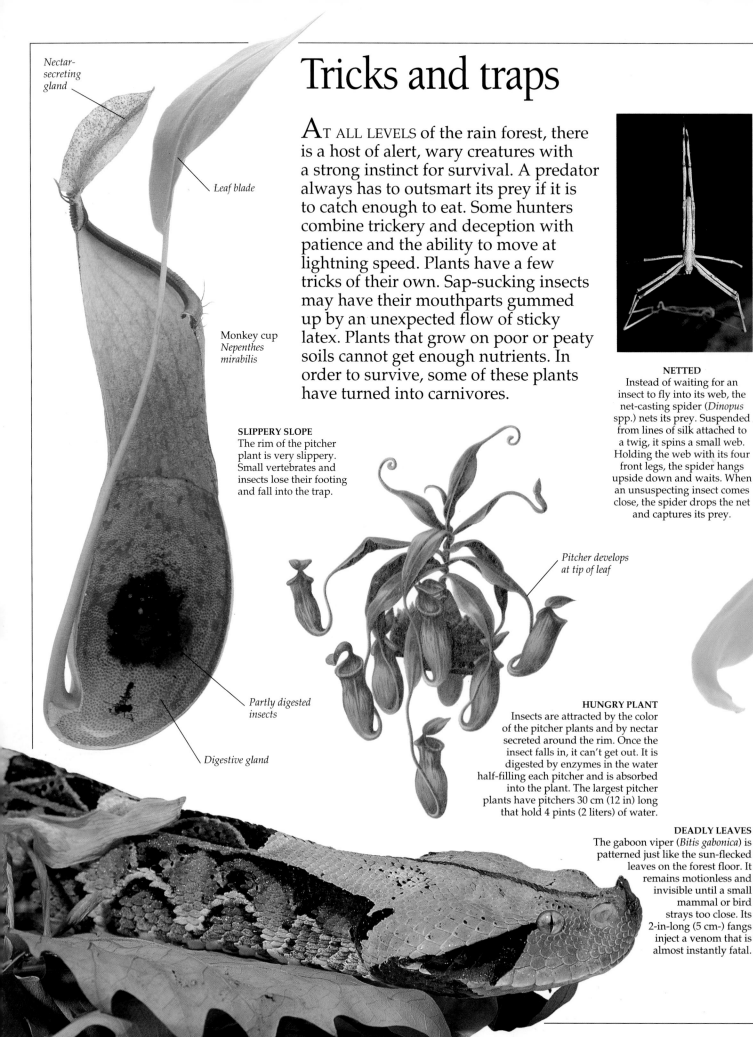

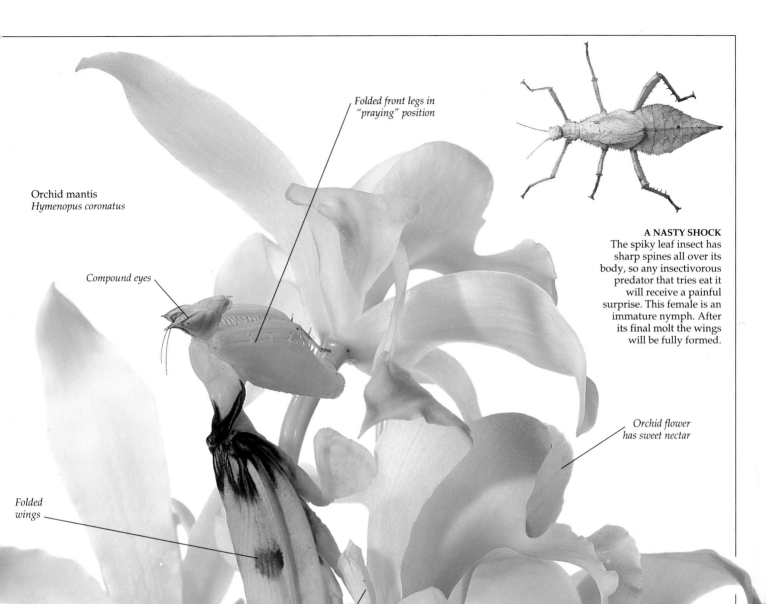

Orchid mantis
Hymenopus coronatus

Folded front legs in "praying" position

Compound eyes

Folded wings

Flap on back leg

A NASTY SHOCK
The spiky leaf insect has sharp spines all over its body, so any insectivorous predator that tries eat it will receive a painful surprise. This female is an immature nymph. After its final molt the wings will be fully formed.

Orchid flower has sweet nectar

LADY IN WAITING
With her pale creamy color and the petal-like flaps on her legs, this female orchid mantis seems to be part of the spray of blooms. She has two large compound eyes at the corners of a triangular head that swivel around while the rest of her body stays still. When an insect visits the orchid, the mantis takes deadly aim and strikes out with her front legs.

Flying high

FROG BEETLE
This Malayan frog beetle (*Sagra buqueti*) has its wings folded under wing cases called elytra.

BEETLING ABOUT
Before flying, this leaf beetle (*Doryphorella langsdorfii*) opens its elytra and spreads its wings.

LIVING IN THE CANOPY many yards above the ground is fine until an animal needs to travel from one treetop to the next in search of food or to escape a predator. Running down one tree trunk, along the ground, and up the next is hazardous and a waste of energy. Traveling through the air overcomes this, but only birds, bats, and insects have the wings and muscles that permit controlled flight. However, an assortment of other creatures have evolved ways of gliding through the air by increasing their body area, often with flaps of skin. When airborne, these flaps spread out like parachutes, increasing their wind resistance and slowing down the rate of descent. This prevents a damaging collision with the ground below. Many of these gliders can alter direction in midair by moving their legs, tail, or body, and some travel remarkable distances in this way.

BIRDS OF PARADISE
The splendid plumage of male birds of paradise is used simply to attract a mate. Males gather in groups called leks in order to display. Some choose a high treetop and, as day breaks, give a colorful display, flashing their bright, iridescent plumage, while making loud calls.

FLYING GECKO
This nocturnal gecko (*Ptychozoon kuhli*) lives in trees and relies on camouflage to hide it from predators. If it is spotted, it escapes by launching itself into the air and gliding to safety. Loose flaps of skin along each side of its body, and smaller flaps on its legs, spread out and fill with air.

Wide scales along tail

Flaps make lizard wider and flatter for gliding

Long legs for running

FLYING FROG
The Malaysian flying frog (*Rhacophorus reinwardii*) is one of a small number of rain forest tree frogs that leap out of a tree to escape from a pursuer. The digits of their very large hands and feet are connected by webs of skin. During long gliding leaps, these webs of skin serve as parachutes.

HUNTING WASP
The electric blue female hunting wasp (*Chlorion lobatum*) cruises low over the forest floor, hunting for crickets. It grips its prey with powerful jaws and paralyzes it with venom injected by its stinger. It drags the insect into a burrow and lays a single egg in it so that, on hatching, the larva has food until it pupates.

Webbing between toes

Blue-and-yellow macaw
Ara ararauna
(South America)

EXPERT PILOTS

Macaws have short, broad wings so that they can skillfully maneuver between the leafy branches of the forest canopy. They fly considerable distances in search of trees bearing ripe fruits. By changing the position of their wings and tail feathers, they can glide and brake before landing on a branch or at a tree-hole nesting site.

FLYING SNAKE

The flying tree snake (*Chrysopelea pelias*) is one of five species from Southeast Asia that can glide through the air. By raising its ribs upward and outward, the snake flattens its body and manages to travel distances of up to 165 ft (50 m) from one tree to another.

Flying dragon
Draco spp.

FLYING LIZARD

Flying dragons have six or seven pairs of elongated ribs covered with a membrane of skin. These "wings" fold up against the lizard's body, but open out so it can glide long distances.

Wing pattern and colors help males and females find each other

GIANT MOTH

The Atlas moth (*Attacus atlas*) is one of the largest moths, with a wingspan of 10-12 in (25-30 cm). Unlike those of other insects, the wings of moths and butterflies are covered with minute, overlapping scales. These are richly colored, some because they contain colored pigments, others because of the way that they reflect the light that falls on them.

Australasian rain forests

ONE HUNDRED MILLION years ago, Australia was part of Antarctica, and rain forest covered the moist coastal regions of this vast southern continent. As Australia separated and drifted north, it became drier, and Antarctica colder. Australia's rain forests are all that is left of this ancient jungle, and contain some primitive flowering plants and conifers. Apart from the bats, all the native animals are pouch-bearing marsupials. New Guinea is to the north, a heavily forested island with a mixture of Asian and Australian plants and animals.

DANGER UNDERFOOT
The marbled scorpion (*Lychas marmoreus*) is found under bark and among leaf litter, where it hunts for small invertebrates. It usually overpowers its victims with its front claws and jaws. The venomous sting in the tail is used primarily for defense.

RARE AND BEAUTIFUL
Living only in a small area of the extreme southeast of Papua New Guinea, this is one of the world's rarest butterflies. It is also the largest—the female has a wingspan of up to 11 in (28 cm). These butterflies are found in the forest margins, but little is known about them.

The male is smaller than the female

Queen Alexandra's birdwing
Ornithoptera alexandrae

GREEN AND RED
The tiny flowers of this fig (*Ficus racemosus*) are contained in the fleshy green swellings that will eventually become sweet fruits. When the figs ripen, they turn red.

IN THE SHADE
This fleshy-stemmed fern lives beside water in shady forests. There is little strengthening tissue in the leaf stalks, and they soon wilt in dry conditions. *Angiopteris* ferns are very similar to the primitive ferns and tree ferns that were alive 325 to 280 million years ago, in the Upper Carboniferous period.

Long, arching leaf stalk

Marattia fern
Angiopteris lygodiifolia

SOGERI SING-SING
In Papua New Guinea elaborate rituals and ceremonies such as the sing-sings have always been an important part of tribal life. New Guinea men adorn themselves with brightly colored body paints, feathers, shells, and beads. Head-dresses made with bird of paradise feathers are especially prestigious.

Doria's tree kangaroo
Dendrolagus dorianus

UP A TREE

Tree kangaroos have evolved from ground-living ancestors. They climb trees to browse on the foliage, but most kinds can still hop over the ground. Doria's tree kangaroo is the most arboreal. It has strong forelegs, broad hind feet, and sharp claws, and it can no longer hop like other kangaroos. It lives in the cooler forests of the New Guinea highlands and has a thick fur coat to keep warm.

Sharp claws for climbing

New Guinea

AUSTRALIA

☐ *Former rain forest*
◻ *Actual rain forest*

AUSTRALASIA

New Guinea contains the largest expanse of rain forest to be found in Southeast Asia. Most of it is still undisturbed, and many remote regions have yet to be explored. In contrast, Australian tropical rain forests are limited to patches in three main areas along the northeast coastal region .

FRIENDLY FROG

White's tree frog (*Litoria caerulea*) has round toe pads that are sticky with mucus. It lives in forests, although it is familiar to many Australians because it also lives in water barrels and lavatories. It is 2-4 in (6-11 cm) long, and feeds on any moving creature small enough to swallow. These frogs spawn in still water, producing 200 to 2,000 eggs.

STICKY MEDICINE

The small tree *Ervatamia orientalis* grows in clearings and at the edges of Australian rain forests. When broken, the stems ooze a white milky latex that some Aborigines use to treat wounds and sores.

Jungle produce

F OR MANY CENTURIES, jungle products have been carried all around the world. A few, such as rubber, sugar, and chocolate, are now so much a part of everyday life it is easy to forget their rain forest origins. Products sold all over the world are grown mostly in plantations. However, some, such as Brazil nuts, are still gathered from the forest. Many of the fruits and seeds that the native peoples have enjoyed for a long time are only now beginning to find new markets in North America and Europe. In the future, we may be enjoying ice creams and using cosmetics that contain ever more exotic ingredients from the jungle.

NUTMEG PLANT
The red aril around the nutmeg seed is also used as a spice called mace.

Ginger
Zingiber officinale

SPICING IT UP
Strongly flavored spices such as pepper, ginger, cloves, and nutmeg were highly prized and very expensive in Europe in the Middle Ages. They were used to hide the tainted flavor of bad meat. Today, they are used to enhance the flavor of food, and to make medicines and toothpastes taste better. Spices are prepared from different parts of plants. For example, nutmeg is a seed, cloves are unopened flower buds, cinnamon comes from bark, and ginger is a root. Spices are dried and can be ground into a powder.

Cloves
Syzygium aromaticum

Nutmeg
Myristica fragrans

Cinnamon
Cinnamomum zeylanicum

A POPULAR FLAVOR
Over 1,227,000 tons of cocoa beans are produced every year to manufacture chocolate, cocoa, and cocoa butter.

COCOA BEANS
Cocoa trees have been cultivated for over 2,000 years in Central America. The Aztecs called the pods "cacahual," and believed that Quetzalcoatl, the plumed serpent god, dined on them. When ripe, cocoa pods are cut and split open by hand. The wet, pulpy mass of seeds is piled into baskets and allowed to ferment to lose unwanted pulp and develop the flavor. Then the seeds – the cocoa beans – are dried, cleaned, and polished, ready for export.

Cocoa pod
Theobroma cacao

Pulp

Rows of 20-60 oval seeds are embedded in a sweet pulp

Starfruit
Averrhoa carambola

Pineapple
Ananas comosus

STARFRUIT
Starfruits grow wild in Indonesian forests, but are planted widely in tropical Asia. They are an attractive garnish on food, as well as a source of vitamin C and iron.

SWEET POTATO
This starchy root (*Ipomoea batatas*) originated in tropical America and contains sugars, so it is pleasantly sweet. Sweet potatoes are boiled, roasted, or dried and ground into flour.

BREADFRUIT
The mass of flowers on this plant develop into the breadfruit, which is 8-12 in (20-30 cm) across and can weigh as much as 4 lb 4 oz (2 kg). Its moist, starchy flesh is cooked as a vegetable.

RUBBER
Over 1,000 kinds of plants produce the white, sticky latex that can be made into rubber. The para rubber tree (*Hevea brasiliensis*) is by far the most commonly used.

Pineapple cloth, or piña

PINEAPPLE
Originating in South America, pineapples are now grown in many tropical countries. Both fresh and canned pineapples are popular foods, but the leaves have a different use. In the Philippines, thin fibers are extracted, prepared, spun, and woven by hand to make a fine sheer cloth called piña. Piña shirts are part of the national costume.

Breadfruit
Artocarpus altilis

59

Explorers

Large, sturdy prehensile tail

THE PROFITABLE spice market drew Portuguese, English, and Dutch explorers to the forested islands of Southeast Asia in the 15th, 16th, and 17th centuries. At the same time, Spanish conquistadors were exploring Central America and Peru, interested more in ransacking Aztec and Inca gold than in the jungles. From the 16th century onward, rival European nations fought to extend their empires in tropical regions. The 18th and 19th centuries saw a steady rise in scientific curiosity about these areas, with explorers such as Darwin and Wallace evolving the theories that have shaped modern thinking.

WILLIAM BLIGH (1754-1817)
For explorers who sailed the seas in bygone days, conditions were harsh. In 1789, Captain Bligh was skipper of the *Bounty*, commissioned to transport young breadfruit trees from the islands of Tahiti to the West Indies. His crew, who wanted to stay on Tahiti, rebelled, and the famous mutiny took place. A second attempt to deliver the trees succeeded and one, planted by Bligh on St. Vincent, is still standing.

AIMÉ BONPLAND (1773-1858)
With von Humboldt, the Frenchman Aimé Bonpland explored both montane and lowland rain forests. Bonpland was a gifted artist and botanist, and recorded over 3,000 new species of plant, such as this *Melastoma coccinea*, in a splendid series of paintings.

Simia ursina painted by Alexander von Humboldt

ALEXANDER VON HUMBOLDT (1769-1859)
This German naturalist landed in Venezuela in 1799, with Bonpland. Von Humboldt had a keen scientific interest in the animals, plants, and places he discovered.

IT'S ALL IN THE NAME
This woolly monkey, *Lagothrix lagotricha* (left), comes from the Orinoco and Upper Amazon basins. It is often called Humboldt's monkey to commemorate the intrepid explorer, who had to put up with swarms of biting insects and fevers in this very humid region.

Livingstone's compass

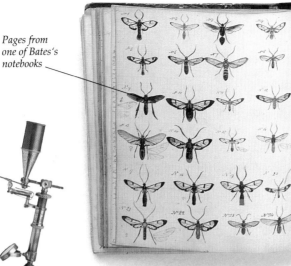
Pages from one of Bates's notebooks

DAVID LIVINGSTONE (1813-1873)
Livingstone, a Scotsman, traveled to Africa to combine his missionary calling with exploration of "the interior". He made three expeditions, traveling by river and mapping the Zambesi River and parts of the Nile.

CHARLES DARWIN (1809-1882)
Abandoning medicine and the priesthood, Darwin joined the crew of the *Beagle* in 1831. He was hired to record wildlife found during the ship's mission to chart the South American coastline. The observations he made formed the basis for his theory of evolution.

Darwin's microscope

HENRY BATES (1825-1892)
In 1848, Henry Bates and his friend Alfred Wallace left England to explore the Amazon. In 11 years, Bates collected 14,000 specimens, mostly insects, of which 8,000 were new to science. He described how some harmless species mimic poisonous ones; this is now known as Batesian mimicry.

BRINGING IT HOME
Transporting specimens back from the rainforests has always been difficult. This early 20th-century Wardian case (left) is a portable greenhouse used to carry plants safely back to the Royal Botanic Gardens in Kew, England. Plant specimens were also preserved by being pressed flat between sheets of absorbent paper. Succulent plants and fruits were preserved in spirits to stop them from getting moldy.

Glass roof like greenhouse

YOUNG VENTURER
Since the 1970s, Colonel John Blashford-Snell has probably done most to enable biologists and young people called Venturers to investigate the canopy. In Operations Drake and Raleigh, the biologists and Venturers studied plants and animals from lightweight aluminium walkways many feet above the ground.

Under threat

EVERY YEAR BETWEEN ONE AND TWO PERCENT of the world's rainforest is cleared. The trees may be felled, often illegally, for logs and to clear land for farming. Some areas of rainforest have been polluted by mining activities. New roads have opened up once inaccessible regions, and people settling alongside them clear more land to grow crops. Conserving rainforests is one of the biggest challenges for environmentalists. At the current rate of deforestation, some scientists estimate that 17,000 species of rainforest plants and animals become extinct every year.

CLEARANCE FOR CATTLE RANCHING
In South and Central America, cleared tropical rainforest provides pasture for beef cattle. When ranchers move into the forest, they burn trees to clear the land for farming. After five years, each animal needs 12.5 acres (5 hectares) to graze. After 10 years the land is useless. Overgrazing, the impact of the animals' hooves, and the loss of the trees lead to soil erosion.

ENVIRONMENTAL INFLUENCES
Rainforests influence the carbon cycle and have a profound effect on rainfall. The uneven surface of treetops causes air turbulence that increases the amount of water evaporating from the forest. This forms clouds that fall as rain. If the forests disappear, less rain will fall, it will drain more quickly, and air and soil temperatures will rise.

CO_2 removed from air during photosynthesis

CO_2 released into air during respiration of tree

Carnivore feeds on other animals

Leaves, branches, and trunk built up from carbon-containing compounds

Droppings and remains from carnivorous animals

CO_2 released by respiring animals

Droppings and remains from herbivorous animals

Falling leaves and branches

CO_2 released from droppings and remains by decomposition

CO_2 released from leaf litter by fungi and invertebrates

Swallow-tailed manakin
Chiroxiphia caudata
(South and Central America)

THE CARBON CYCLE
Green plants take up carbon dioxide, which they convert to sugars by means of photosynthesis. During this process, oxygen is released into the air.

VULNERABLE
Manakins live in the thickest forests and are not endangered at present. But their lifestyle and specialized diet of small soft fruits makes them vulnerable to forest disturbance.

THE OLD AND THE NEW
This beautiful Dutch mahogany armoire is an antique. Today, most of the mahogany that comes from Amazonia is poached – felled illegally – at the expense of the lives and livelihood of the Amerindian tribespeople.

EMBROIDERED CLOTH, NILGIRI HILLS
In the Nilgiri Hills, in India, a large area
of forest has been made into a Biosphere
Reserve. Tribal groups are encouraged
to live there in a traditional way, and
they supplement their livelihood
by making items for export.

*Maxillaria
fulgens*
(Central
America)

WIGMAN OF THE HULI TRIBE
Papua New Guinea has some of the least
disturbed areas of rain forest. Many
tribes live there, but the harmony with
their surroundings is easily disrupted.

OBSESSIVE COLLECTION
Many of the estimated
18,000 species of orchid
are found in rain forests.
Their exotic blooms attract
collectors, and the trade
in these flowers, although
frequently illegal, is worth
a lot of money. Orchids
are highly susceptible to
over-collection, and some
face extinction in the wild.

Orangutan
Pongo pygmaeus
(Southeast Asia)

*Arms are much
longer than legs*

*Short fifth toe to
help grip branches
when swinging*

NOWHERE TO LIVE
Selective logging removes
target trees but leaves the rest.
The increased light stimulates
new growth, which benefits some
animals, such as leaf-eating
primates that prefer young foliage.
Others are not so adaptable. The
adult orangutan forages over a
wide area on its own and is highly
sensitive to disturbance. Like
all other jungle creatures, this "man
of the forest" has a right to survive.

Did you know?

Amazon River

Golden arrow poison frog

Two and a half acres (one hectare) of jungle can support around 100 different kinds of tree. Some tropical forests have more than 300.

In the South American rain forest, one scientist discovered around 50 species of ants in one square meter of leaf litter.

A rain forest's canopy is so dense that it blocks out about 98 percent of the Sun's light. Most animals live in this part of the forest.

A sloth's fur has a green tinge because of the algae growing on it. Because a sloth spends most of its time hanging upside down, its fur is parted along its stomach rather than its back (as on other animals) to allow rainwater to run off.

About 7,800 square miles (20,200 square kilometers) of rain forest are lost every year—that's an area the size of New Jersey.

One quarter of all medicines used today are derived from plants. Drugs used to treat cancer, Hodgkin's disease, and other forms of leukemia all come from rain-forest plants.

Rain-forest orchid
Odontoglossom laeve

Rain forests cover just 6 percent of the Earth's total land area, yet are home to more than half the plant and animal species living on Earth.

Half of the world's rain forests are within the borders of just three countries: Brazil in South America, Indonesia in Southeast Asia, and Zaire in Africa.

Tropical rain forests have an average temperature of around 77°F (25°C).

Motionless potoo guarding single egg in nest

The golden arrow poison frog found in the South American rain forest has enough venom in its skin to kill 950 people.

During the day, the common potoo of Central and South America camouflages itself by sitting in an upright posture, often on a broken branch or tree stump, with its head and bill pointing to the sky so it looks like part of the tree. It hunts for food at night.

Some treetop bromeliads can hold up to 12 gallons (55 liters) of water (about 8 sinkfuls!), providing a home to frogs, snakes, spiders, and even small mammals.

Up to 80 different species of plant may live on a single emergent rain-forest tree.

Most of the world's 18,000–20,000 species of orchid live in tropical forests.

Camouflaged potoo

QUESTIONS AND ANSWERS

Q Why are rain-forest trees important to the Earth's climate?

A Trees in the rain forest—like all green plants—use carbon dioxide and produce oxygen when they make food from sunlight through photosynthesis. It is estimated that rain forests produce 50 percent of the Earth's oxygen. However, the main reason they affect our climate is that they hold vast stores of carbon in their leaves, stems, and roots. When they are burned or cut down and left to rot to clear land, the stored carbon is released into the atmosphere as carbon dioxide gas, contributing to the Greenhouse Effect.

Q Will the rain-forest trees regrow if they are cut down?

A If left undisturbed, rain forests will gradually regrow. However, it is doubtful whether they will ever support the same variety of plants and animals. Regrowth happens naturally in forests when large trees die and fall to the ground, often taking smaller trees with them. As light pours into the "gap," fast-growing seeds and saplings grow upward, with one tree eventually outgrowing the rest. If huge areas of rain forest are cut down, however, the unprotected soil is eroded through heavy rains. Although new plants take root and grow, tall trees are unlikely to have enough soil and nutrients to grow into giants.

Cassowary of the Australasian rain forest

Collecting latex

Q Why do more types of animals live in rain forests than in any other habitat?

A Rain forests have existed for millions of years—some Southeast Asian rain forests are around 100 million years old—so animals have had plenty of time to evolve. Conditions in the rain forests, with constant temperatures and plenty of rainfall, are ideal for sustaining a variety of animal life. Animals do not need to adapt to find ways to survive cold winters or to keep out of the hot sun, and they always have enough water.

Rain forest in Ecuador, cleared for oil exploration

Q What is sustainable farming and can it help save the rain forests?

A Sustainable use of the forest is the harvesting of rain-forest products without affecting the rain forest's delicate balance of nature. For example, the Brazilian government has set aside land in which Brazil nuts can be harvested from the wild in a way that does not require deforestation. Similarly, latex can be collected from rubber trees without mass deforestation. These schemes not only help to save rain-forest trees, they also provide an income for indigenous peoples. However, much more needs to be done. Wood is a renewable resource and many environmental groups now back schemes for the sustainable use of the world's forests.

Record Breakers

LARGEST JUNGLE BIRD
The cassowary of the Australasian rain forest grows up to 5 ft (1.5 m) tall.

LARGEST JUNGLE FLOWER
The giant rafflesia of Southeast Asia can grow around 3 ft (1 m) wide and weigh up to 15.4 lb (7 kg).

Rafflesia

LARGEST BUTTERFLY
The Queen Alexandra's birdwing has a wingspan of up to 11 in (28 cm).

LONGEST JUNGLE SNAKE
The anaconda of South America grows to an average length of 18 ft (5.5 m).

Endangered jungle animals

HERE ARE JUST A FEW RAIN-FOREST ANIMALS that are endangered because of poaching and loss of habitat. Some are now critically endangered, meaning they face an extremely high risk of extinction in the wild.*

Philippine eagle

Common gibbon

AYE AYE
Daubentonia madagascariensis
Habitat and range: Protected rain forest on the African island of Madagascar
Status: Endangered
Numbers: Estimated population of fewer than 2,500; numbers are expected to halve over the next 10 years based on current rate of habitat loss.
Reasons for decline: Habitat loss through logging and conversion to agriculture; the aye aye has also often been killed by local people who consider a sighting of the animal to be a harbinger of misfortune.

Aye aye

PHILIPPINE EAGLE
Pithecophages jefferyi
Habitat and range: Rain forests in Indonesia and the Philippines (the eagle is the national bird of the Philippines)
Status: Critically endangered
Numbers: There are thought to be possibly fewer than 250 mature birds in the wild; attempts are now being made to breed the eagle in captivity and return it to its natural habitat.
Reasons for decline: Erosion of habitat through logging and clearing land for agriculture.

Long arms for swinging and reaching fruit

JAVAN SILVERY GIBBON
Hylobates moloch
Habitat and range: Rain forest of western and central Java in Southeast Asia
Status: Critically endangered
Numbers: There are thought to be just 2,000 Javan gibbons in fragmented populations in the wild. Other species of gibbon, such as the common (or lars) gibbon, are currently considered low risk because there are around 300,000 remaining in their native habitat. However, if current rates of deforestation continue, they may also become vulnerable and even endangered with extinction.
Reasons for decline: Loss of habitat through deforestation for farming, logging, and mining

Sumatran tiger

SUMATRAN ORANGUTAN
Pongo abelii
Habitat and range: Rain forests of Sumatra in Southeast Asia
Status: Critically endangered
Numbers: There are thought to be just 15,000 to 20,000 orangutans (*Pongo pygmaeus* and *Pongo abelii*) remaining in the wild.
Reasons for decline: Poaching and loss of habitat; some animals are also captured for the illegal pet trade.

SUMATRAN TIGER
Panthera tigris ssp *sumatrae*
Habitat and range: Sumatran forest, including tropical forest
Status: Endangered
Numbers: There are thought to be only around 400 animals remaining in the wild, in Sumatra's five national parks.
Reasons for decline: Loss of habitat, poaching, and the illegal trade in tiger parts for use in traditional Chinese medicine. The other three subspecies of tiger are also endangered.

Adult orangutans are solitary animals, ranging over several miles of rain forest.

* Based on data from the 2002 Red List of Threatened Species™. For up-to-date information, log on to www.redlist.org/

Sumatran orangutan

Bonobo

BONOBO (PYGMY CHIMPANZEE)
Pan paniscus
Habitat and range: Remote rain forests of central Zaire in Africa
Status: Endangered (along with other kinds of chimpanzee, such as the western chimpanzee)
Numbers: Estimates suggest there are 10,000–15,000 left in the wild.
Reasons for decline: Hunting for its meat and the sale of young as pets

GORILLA
Gorilla gorilla
Habitat: Central Africa, in small areas of wild forest and reserves
Status: All gorillas (eastern, western, and mountain) are now endangered.
Numbers: There are thought to be around 40,000 western lowland gorillas remaining in the wild. The eastern lowland gorilla, now found only in the Democratic Republic of Congo, is thought to have a population of 3,000–5,000. The mountain gorilla is the most endangered, with only 670 animals remaining in the wild. Half of this number live in protected areas of the Virunga volcanic region of Rwanda, Uganda, and the Democratic Republic of Congo. The rest live in Bwindi National Park in Uganda.
Reasons for decline: Loss of forest home due to logging or clearing land for ranches, farms, and plantations. Civil unrest in some African countries has also made it difficult to patrol reserves and safeguard animals from poachers, who hunt gorillas for their meat and skins. Hunting gorillas and other wild animals in the forests of the Congo Basin in Africa is so excessive that poaching is considered to be more of a threat to animal conservation than deforestation.

Mountain gorilla
from Rwanda

Hyacinth
macaw

HYACINTH MACAW
Anodorhynchus hyacinthinus
Habitat and range: South American rain forest in Brazil, Bolivia, and Paraguay
Status: Endangered
Numbers: Around 2,500–5,000 birds in three distinct populations.
Reasons for decline: Trade (considered a prized pet), hunting, and deforestation

Hunted to extinction

Many countries have passed laws banning the hunting of endangered animals and have set aside national parks and reserves to preserve what remains of their habitats. However, even though it is illegal, many endangered animals, such as the orangutan, tiger, and rhinoceros, are still poached for their meat and hides. Sometimes mothers are killed so that their young can be captured and sold as pets.

Young primates are also caught and sold for medical research. Many endangered animals are also hunted because their body parts are though to have healing powers in traditional Chinese medicine. For example, a tiger's whiskers are sold to ease toothache, its tail is used to treat skin diseases, and its bones are thought to help cure rheumatism.

Rhino horns

SUMATRAN RHINOCEROS
Dicerorhinus sumatrensis
Habitat and range: Lowland rain forests of Southeast Asia
Status: Critically endangered
Numbers: It is estimated that there are fewer than 300 animals remaining in the wild, in the forests of Indonesia and Malaysia. The Javan rhinoceros is also critically endangered, with just 60 animals left in the lowland rain forests of Ujung Kulon National Park on Java, Indonesia, and Cat Tien National Park in Vietnam.
Reasons for decline: Deforestation, and poaching for its highly priced horn, which is thought to have medicinal properties

Sumatran
rhinoceros

Find out more

THERE IS A WEALTH OF INFORMATION AVAILABLE about the world's jungles. Maybe one day you will be fortunate enough to explore a rain forest. Until then, see jungle animals up close in local zoos and wildlife centers, and find out about their captive breeding programs and other important conservation work. You can also watch wildlife shows on television, go online to access information over the Internet, join a conservation group, or visit a botanical garden to learn more.

Golden lion tamarin

ZOOS AND WILDLIFE CENTERS
Find out about your nearest zoo's conservation work. It may be involved in breeding and raising endangered animals. In the 1970s, the golden lion tamarin was thought to be the world's most endangered primate, with only around 100 animals left in the wild. Since then, captive breeding programs in zoos worldwide and the setting up of forest reserves have increased populations, and the golden lion tamarin now has a much greater chance of survival.

ECOTOURISM
It is now easier to visit some of the world's rain forests through ecotourism. Ecotourism means to visit a place to sightsee or learn about its natural environment without, for example, staying in a fancy hotel and using up valuable water resources. While ecotourism in the world's rain forests does not directly help to save the forests, money spent by tourists can be used for conservation work, reforestation, management of reserves, and so on. However, care must be taken not to upset the ecosystem's delicate balance of nature, so tourism must be carefully managed, and visitor numbers are limited.

Ecotourism in Malaysian rain forest

The Dian Fossey
Gorilla Fund
International

Ecotourists in
Rwanda, Africa

ADOPT AN ANIMAL
Many zoos and conservation organizations enable you to adopt an animal by making a contribution toward its upkeep. For example, through the Dian Fossey Gorilla Fund International (an organization that continues the work of Dian Fossey, a scientist who dedicated her life to saving mountain gorillas), you can adopt a gorilla from the Karisoke Research Center in Rwanda. When you adopt an animal you receive a photo and adoption papers and can keep track of the animal on the Web site: http://www.gorillafund.org/

Places to visit

JUNGLE GARDENS AND BIRD SANCTUARY, Avery Island, Louisiana
Jungle Gardens showcases tropical plants, and enormous flocks of herons and egrets rest here in its bird sanctuary in early spring and summer.

SAN DIEGO ZOO, San Diego, California
The San Diego Zoo is active in world conservation efforts. Many endangered jungle animals are on display at the zoo and its wild animal park.

BRONX ZOO, Bronx, New York
The Bronx Zoo is also active in conservation. Visit its indoor Asian rain forest—almost a full acre in size—and its Congo Gorilla habitat.

NATIONAL ZOOLOGICAL PARK, Washington, D.C.
Exhibits at the National Zoo, which works with the Conservation and Research Center Foundation, allow visitors to get close to rare animals.

AMERICAN MUSEUM OF NATURAL HISTORY, New York, New York
A re-creation of the Dzanga-Sangha rain forest takes visitors into the jungle, with tangled vines and branches above and leaf litter concealing insects, reptiles, and ground mammals below.

Rattan palm

LONDON ZOO, REGENT'S PARK, LONDON
Find out about the zoo's work in animal conversation and see:
• Sumatran tigers, which are part of a European captive breeding program
• the Macaw Aviary, including endangered hyacinth macaws

WHIPSNADE WILD ANIMAL PARK, BEDFORDSHIRE
This wildlife park has over 2,500 animals living in open paddocks or roaming free in parkland. Look for the three species of rhinoceros (black, white, and Asian) threatened with extinction, now bred in the park.

CONSERVATION MATTERS

Contact an environmental group to see what it is doing to try to save and protect the world's rain forests and find out how you can help. Many of these groups have Web sites (see box below) and produce information such as factsheets, films, and brochures. They also raise money and campaign for stricter environmental laws. Help save rain-forest trees by using less paper. As well as recycling paper, write on both sides of every sheet you use, and try to use cloth napkins and towels instead of paper napkins and towels.
Check out the Rainforest Action website (www.ran.org) for plenty of information on recycling as well as wood-free paper options using waste straw, kenaf, or hemp.

Recycling newspapers and magazines

USEFUL WEB SITES

▸ Homepage of the World Wildlife Fund, with information on where to join and other WWF sites: **wwf.org/**
• Learn about the Save-an-Acre program and more at the Web site of Tropical Rainforest Coalition: **www.rainforest.org**
• Rainforest Alliance's site offers an Adopt-a-Rainforest program and features rain-forest photographs and art: **www.therainforestsite.com**
• See photographs from a Smithsonian photographer's six-year documentary of the Panamanian jungle: **photo2.si.edu/crane/craneport.html**

Hexagons in the domed roof are made up of layers of inflated transparent foil, each 6 ft (2 m) deep.

EDEN PROJECT
The Humid Tropics Biome at the Eden Project in Cornwall, England, is the largest conservatory in the world, containing more than 1,000 plant species from the jungles of Malaysia, West Africa, the islands of Oceania, and South America. Misters and waterfalls inside the dome keep the air moist, and the air is regulated so it is between 64.4°–95°F (18°–35°C), re-creating the heat and humidity of a tropical forest. As well as experiencing what it is like to walk through jungle plants, you can also learn about the hundreds of uses of plants in our everyday lives. More information about the Eden Project and news about current exhibitions and workshops can be found on its Web site (www.edenproject.com).

Queen Alexandra birdwing butterfly

BUTTERFLY GARDENS
Large butterfly gardens often have a tropical hothouse where you can see colorful rain-forest species flitting through the trees. The London Butterfly House at Syon Park, Brentford, has 500–1200 butterflies, with species from Costa Rica, Indonesia, Thailand, and the Philippines.

Inside the Humid Tropics Biome at the Eden Project

Glossary

ADAPTATION Process by which a living organism gradually changes genetically so that is becomes better suited to a particular environment

AMPHIBIAN Ectothermic (cold-blooded) vertebrate such as a frog, whose young use gills to breathe during the early stages of life

BIODIVERSITY (or biological diversity) The wide variety of living organisms, including plant and animal life

BIOME Large ecological unit broadly corresponding to one of the world's major climatic regions, such as a tropical forest, desert, and so on

BIOSPHERE All the habitats on Earth

BROMELIAD Member of a family of plants, many of which are epiphytes that live on the boughs of trees (*see also* EPIPHYTE)

BUTTRESS ROOT Supporting structure that grows from the base of a tree's trunk, helping to support its weight

CAMOUFLAGE An animal's color or pattern that enables it to blend in with its surroundings in order to hide from predators or lie in wait for prey

CANOPY Layer in a forest that is made up of the leafy crowns of most trees

CARBON DIOXIDE Colorless, odorless gas given out by animals and plants during respiration, which is absorbed by plants during photosynthesis. Too much carbon dioxide gas in the atmosphere results in global warming. (*see also* GLOBAL WARMING)

Bromeliad

CARNAUBA Type of high-quality wax taken from wax palms, used mainly in the cosmetics and polishes industries

CINCHONA Plant from which quinine is obtained, which is sometimes used in the treatment of malaria

CLIMATE The pattern of weather in a particular place over a long period of time

CLOUD FOREST Type of rain forest growing at high altitudes, enveloped by permanent heavy mist, and usually covered by a thick layer of moss and liverwort

CONSERVATION Protecting, preserving, and managing the Earth's natural resources and its environment

CURARE Type of poison used by some South American tribespeople to coat their arrow tips when hunting prey

CYCAD Palm-like, seed-bearing plant with long fern-like leaves

DEFORESTATION When forest is felled

Emergent tree breaking through the canopy

and cleared as a result of human activity

ECOLOGY The scientific study of plants and animals in relation to their environment, or ecosystem

ECOSYSTEM A community of living organisms in their natural habitat, forming an interdependent food chain (*see also* BIOME)

EMERGENT Very tall tree that towers above the rest of the rain forest canopy (*see also* CANOPY)

ENDANGERED In danger of extinction

EPIPHYTE Plant that grows on another plant (often a tree) for support, and often to reach the light. Epiphytes absorb nutrients from rain and debris lodged on the bark of the tree.

EXTINCTION The dying out of a plant or animal species

FOOD CHAIN Series of plants and animals linked by their feeding relationships

Kapok fiber

Kapok pod

FOOD WEB A series of several interlinked food chains

GERMINATION Process in which a seed starts to grow

GLOBAL WARMING Warming of the Earth's atmosphere caused by a build-up of greenhouse gases (*see also* CARBON DIOXIDE, GREENHOUSE EFFECT)

GREENHOUSE EFFECT The accumulation of gases such as carbon dioxide in the atmosphere, which allows sunlight to reach the Earth's surface but prevents heat from escaping

Primate

HABITAT Environment or surroundings in which an organism (plant or animal) lives

HUMIDITY The amount of water vapor in the air. A tropical rain forest has an average humidity of around 82 percent

HUMUS Decomposed organic matter

KAPOK Light, waterproof, oily fiber covering the seeds of some species of silk-cotton tree; often used for stuffing pillows

LATEX Thick, milky juice produced by some plants, including the rubber tree, the sap of which is used in the manufacture of rubber products

LIANA Plant with a long, slender stem that climbs or twines up jungle trees or dangles down from the canopy so its leaves can reach the light.

LICHEN Plantlike organism formed from a partnership between a fungus and an alga or cyanobacterium, which forms crusts and tufts on trees, rocks, or soil

LITTER Dead leaves, twigs, and branches that fall to, and carpet, the forest floor

LIVERWORT Plant related to moss; some have a lobed plant-body that resembles a liver; once used to treat liver diseases

MAMMAL Endothermic (warm-blooded), hairy vertebrate that suckles its young

MANGROVE Tree that grows in muddy swamps covered at high tide, or on tropical coasts and the shores of estuaries; characterized by long, tangled roots

MARSUPIAL Animal in which the young is usually carried in a pouch by the female

MIMICRY Copying the behavior, coloring, or markings of another more dangerous animal to escape from predators

MONSOON Wind that changes direction according to the seasons; also used to mean the heavy seasonal rains it brings to parts of the world

MOSS Small plant with simply constructed leaves attaching itself to the earth, trees, or rock by short, rootlike hairs.

NOCTURNAL Active by night rather than by day (diurnal)

NUTRIENT Food needed by plants and animals to live and grow

POACHER Hunter who kills an animal illegally. Some commercial poachers use shotguns, rifles, or even machine guns to kill their prey. Others use more traditional weapons, such as spears or arrows.

PHOTOSYNTHESIS The process by which green plants produce food by using the energy from sunlight to build simple sugars from carbon dioxide and water

PREHENSILE Flexible part of the body (usually the tail) that is able to grip. For example, some monkeys have prehensile tails, which are used like another hand to hold branches.

PRESERVATION Keeping something from harm or decay

Liana

Tendril

PRIMATE An order in the animal kingdom that includes monkeys, apes, and human beings

REPTILE Ectothermic (cold-blooded), scaly vertebrate (animal with a backbone) that reproduces by laying eggs or giving birth on land. Living reptiles include lizards, snakes, turtles, and crocodiles.

SLASH AND BURN AGRICULTURE When land is cleared by slashing trees and bushes then burning them to release nutrients into the soil. The cleared land is usually used for farming or for raising cattle.

SPECIES A distinct group of plants or animals that can breed successfully with a member of the same group to produce fertile offspring

STILT ROOT Long root growing from the lower part of a trunk, giving a plant support on difficult terrain, such as steep slopes

STRANGLER FIG Type of plant that starts life as an epiphyte, growing on a treetop branch. Its long aerial roots eventually grow down to the ground, covering the tree until the tree dies and rots away.

TENDRIL Coiled shoot from a climbing plant that enables it to cling to another plant and climb toward the light

TRANSPIRATION Release of water into the air from green plants during the process of photosynthesis (making food from sunlight)

TROPICAL Related to the tropics—the hot, wet regions lying on or near the equator, between the Tropic of Cancer that lies on the line of latitude 23.5° north of the equator, and the Tropic of Capricorn that lies on the line of latitude 23.5° south of the equator

Tuber of a sweet potato

TUBER Swollen root or underground stem-tip that contains a reserve of food (usually sugars and starches)

UNDERSTORY Layer of vegetation below the rain-forest canopy where limited sunlight penetrates

VENOM Toxic liquid used by an animal to paralyze or kill its prey

Index

Acknowledgments

The publisher would like to thank:
Mark Alcock; the staff of the Royal Botanic Gardens, Kew, in particular Jenny Evans, Doris Francis, Sandra Bell, Phil Brewster, Dave Cooke, John Lonsdale, Mike Marsh, and John Norris; David Field and Sue Brodie of ECOS, the Royal Botanic Gardens, Kew; Mark O'Shea, herpetologist, and Nik Brown and Pete Montague of the West Midland Safari Park; the staff and keepers of Twycross Zoo, in particular Molly Badham, Donna Chester, and John Ray; Robert Opie, Jim Hamill, Jane Beamish, and Mike Row, British Museum, Museum of Mankind; Martin Brendell of the Natural History Museum; Janet Boston of the Liverpool Museum; Helena Spiteri for editorial help; Susan St Louis, Isaac Zamora, Ivan Finnegan, and Sarah Cowley for design help.
Maps by John Woodcock
Additional photography by Peter Anderson (38–39); Geoff Brightling (33tr); Jane Burton/Kim Taylor (17cl and cr, 33cl); Peter Chadwick (16cr); Frank Greenaway (12tl, 23tr and br, 28tl and bl, 29tl, 35cl, 37r, 52b, 53b, 54c, 55b, 56cr); Colin Keates (7cr, 54tl); Dave King (58b); Cyril Laubscher (7tr); Karl Shone (32–33, 62bl); Kim Taylor (40tr, 50–51); Jerry Young (16cl, 17b, 23br, 29bl, 31tr, 35tl, 53tr, 63b)

Index by Hilary Bird

The publisher would like to thank the following for their kind permission to reproduce their photographs:

Picture credits
a-above; b-below; c-center; l-left; r-right; t-top
Bridgeman Art Library/Royal Botanic Gardens, Kew: 18bl, 35c; /Leiden, Rijksmuseum voor Volkenkunde: 38 bc; /British Museum: 39tr; /Royal Geographical Society: 60br; /Bonhams 62bc
Bruce Coleman Ltd: 9tl; /M.P.L.Fogden: 12tr; /G.B.Frith: 15tl; /Konrad Wothe: 16c; /Jane Burton: 27tl; /D.Houston: 28br; /WWF/H.Jungins: 33tl; /Dieter and Mary Plage: 36bl; /Peter Ward: 37bl; /Dieter and Mary Plage: 46tr
Corbis: Michael S. Lewis 68b; Tom Stewart 69tr.
Mary Evans Picture Library: 46tl
Michael & Patricia Fogden: 6bc, 13br, 13bl, 14c, 14tr, 35tr, 51bl, 63tr
Dian Fossey Gorilla Fund International: 68c.
Robert Harding Picture Library: 30lc, 34tr, 39tl, 62tl, 63tc
Hutchison Library /Isabella Tree: 39br; /Dr Nigel Smith: 42br

Frank Lane Picture Agency /E.& D. Hosking: 11tl; /Silvestris: 31bl
Mansell Collection: 60tr
Natural History Museum, London: 59, 69cra.
N.H.P.A.: /Morten Strange: 8tl; /Otto Rogge: 15r; /Stephen Dalton: 24cr, 33cr; /Kevin Schafer: 43tl; /G.I.Bernard: 50cr; /Stephen Kraseman: 50tr; /Alberto Mardi 69br; /Daryl Balfour 67cl; /Gerard Lacz 67br; /Jany Sauvanet 57tc; /Kevin Schafer 70tc; /Mark Bowler 65cr, 66bl; /Martin Wendler 64tl; /Michael Leach 64bl.
N.H.P.A.Planet Earth Pictures: /Andre Bartschi: 8bl; /Peter Scoones: 9tr; /Andrew Mounter: 21tl; /John Lythgoe: 22bl; /Anup Shah: 47br; /David Maitland: 56tr; /Mary Clay: 57bc
Nature Picture Library: /Anup Shah 66br, 67cr; /Bruce Davidson 64-65; /John Cancalosi 71cr; /Morley Read 65b; /Neil Lucas 66tr; /Pete Oxford 66tl; /Staffan Widstrand 71bc; /Stefan Widstrand 70-71; /Sue Daly 64tr.
Oxford Scientific Films: /Harold Taylor 66-67, 70bl; /Konrad Wothe 67tr; /Martyn Colbeck 67tl; /Paul Franklin 68-69; /Philip Tull 68tl; /Steve Turner 71tl.
Panos Pictures /Fred Hoogervorst 68cr.

Premaphotos Wildlife /K.G.Preston-Mafham: 49br, 56lc, 57br
Raleigh International Picture Library /Chris Rainier: 61br
Harry Smith/Polunin Collection: 10tr
Still Pictures /Edward Parker: 6tl; /Norbert Wu: 29tr, 52tr
Survival Anglia /Frances Furlong: 40bc; /M.Kavanagh: 48tr
Syndication International: 58tl; /Natural History Museum: 60cr c.Alan Watson/Forest Light: 8cr
M.I.Walker/Microworld Services: 18bc
Jacket credits:
Front: Mike Hill/Alamy, b; Jerry Young, tr
Back: Natural History Museum, tl, cl; Museum of Mankind, tr

Every effort has been made to trace the copyright holders and we apologize in advance for any unintentional omissions. We would be pleased to insert the appropriate acknowledgment in any subsequent edition of this publication.

All other images © Dorling Kindersley. For further information see: www.dkimages.com